Your Towns and Cities in the Great War

D0541758

Oxford

IN THE GREAT WAR

Your Towns and Cities in the Great War

Oxford
IN THE GREAT WAR

Malcolm Graham

Pen & Sword
MILITARY

First published in Great Britain in 2014 by
Pen & Sword Military
An imprint of
Pen & Sword Books Ltd
47 Church Street
Barnsley
South Yorkshire
S70 2AS

ISBN: 9781783462971

Designed by Factionpress

Printed and bound in England
by Page Bros, Norwich

Pen & Sword Books Ltd incorporates the Imprints of Pen & Sword Aviation,
Pen & Sword Family History, Pen & Sword Maritime, Pen & Sword Military,
Pen & Sword Discovery, Pen & Sword Politics, Pen & Sword Atlas, Pen &
Sword Archaeology, Wharncliffe Local History, Wharncliffe True Crime,
Wharncliffe Transport, Pen & Sword Select, Pen & Sword Military Classics,
Leo Cooper, The Praetorian Press, Claymore Press, Remember When, Seaforth
Publishing and Frontline Publishing.

For a complete list of Pen & Sword titles please contact
PEN & SWORD BOOKS LIMITED
47 Church Street, Barnsley, South Yorkshire, S70 2AS, England
E-mail: enquiries@pen-and-sword.co.uk
Website: www.pen-and-sword.co.uk

Contents

Acknowledgements

Many people have provided invaluable help and advice during the preparation of this book, and I would like to thank the following Oxford college archivists and librarians: Norma Aubertin-Potter, All Souls College; Anna Sander, Balliol College; Elizabeth Boardman, Brasenose College and St Hilda's College; Judith Curthoys, Christ Church; Julian Read, Corpus Christi College and Merton College; Robin Darwall-Smith, Magdalen College and University College; Rob Petre, Oriel College; Michael Riordan, St John's College; Anne Manuel and Kate O'Donnell, Somerville College.

Colin Harris and Mike Webb drew my attention to valuable resources at the Bodleian Libraries, and Simon Bailey, Keeper of the University Archives, and Julie Anne Lambert, Librarian of the John Johnson Collection, kindly facilitated access to those special collections. I am most grateful to Martin Maw, head archivist at Oxford University Press, for making relevant records available, and to Paul Butler, Secretary of Iffley Historical Society, for sharing research about the Iffley Memorial Institute. Stephen Barker, Harry Staff and Stanley Jenkins of the Soldiers of Oxfordshire Trust have also supplied most helpful information.

I am indebted to former colleagues at the Oxfordshire History Centre who have proved equal to my many requests for relevant material; Helen Drury and Mark Lawrence have been particularly supportive in identifying and supplying images. Behind the scenes, my wife Ros has further burnished her credentials by tolerating this latest distraction and helping me to complete the task.

Image Credits:
Master and Fellows of Balliol College, Oxford: 49
Oxfordshire History Centre, Oxfordshire County Council: 1-7, 9-22, 24-26, 28, 30-43, 45-63, 65-80
President and Fellows of St John's College, Oxford: 20
Soldiers of Oxfordshire Trust: 124
Somerville College, University of Oxford: 52
Master and Fellows of University College, Oxford: 57
All the other images are reproduced by kind permission of Oxfordshire History Centre, Oxfordshire County Council.

Introduction

Talk of an Oxford War Museum became public in May 1917. Envisaged as 'a hall of memories' by Robert Buckell, Mayor of Oxford, it would 'record the patriotism and heroism of local inhabitants and the part they had played in the conflict'. The city's War Museum Committee first met in June and agreed that the scope of the museum would include not only citizens who had served in the forces, and, in many cases, given their lives for their country, but also those who had undertaken other war work.

Reports were commissioned about recruiting and tribunals, hospitals, the Oxford Volunteer Force, Food Control, Queen Mary's Needlework Guild, the War Pensions Committee, the YMCA and the Garden Club for wounded soldiers at Mansfield College. Councillor Miss Merivale was asked to obtain information about the work of the women of Oxford. The Oxford photographer, Henry Taunt, was co-

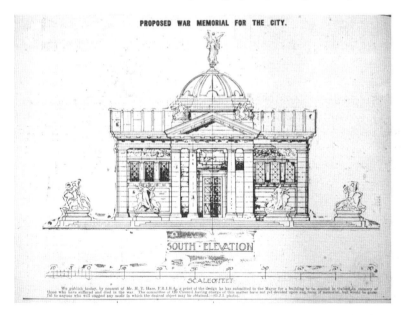

Henry Hare's design for a War Memorial Hall in St Giles', 1919. Nothing came of this scheme for a 'hall of memory', recording Oxford's part in the Great War.

opted on to the committee to help gather in photographs of wartime Oxford. Henry Hare, architect of Oxford's Town Hall, prepared a scheme for a Memorial Hall which would house war relics and a record of the city's role in the Great War.

Nothing came of these ambitious plans. The War Museum Committee was diverted into making plans for a City War Memorial in 1919, and St John's College vetoed the idea of building the Memorial Hall on college land south of St Giles's Church because it would obscure views of the church. The Oxford War Museum never saw the light of day but its ambition to record the sacrifices and experiences of all Oxford citizens, men, women, and children, has been a major inspiration for this book. It is unclear how much the museum would have taken account of the University's contribution to the war effort, but, as W.E. Sherwood, Mayor of Oxford, wrote in 1915: 'We have a crisis in which both City and University and indeed the whole Empire is involved, and we shall sink or swim together.' The role played by the University and Colleges, in Oxford, in the conflict, and across the world, adds a different dimension to the story of a city at war.

The crisis that Sherwood described had swiftly arisen following the assassination of the Archduke Franz Ferdinand, heir to the Austro-Hungarian Empire, and his wife by Gavrilo Princip, a Bosnian Serb, in Sarajevo on 28 June 1914. Through a bewildering chain of events, the pre-existing alliances between Austria and Germany on the one hand, and Great Britain, France and Russia on the other had the fatal effect of locking each country into a war which each could argue to be an act of self-defence. All the participants anticipated a brief struggle, but contemporaries immediately recognised that this was indeed The Great War.

Chapter One

Outbreak of War

OXFORD ON THE EVE OF THE GREAT WAR had a resident population of 53,000, and accommodated some 3,000 undergraduates during University terms. The 1901 Census, taken during the University's Easter vacation, shows that there were more females than males in the city in all age groups over 15. (Appendix Table 1) Living-in domestic servants, especially in North Oxford, accounted for some of this imbalance, and large numbers of women and girls also found work in shops and dressmaking. Oxford also had a significant number of female residents who were living on their own means. (Appendix Table 2) The city was both the market centre for much of Oxfordshire and North Berkshire, and the home of an ancient University with a national and international reputation. This dual role contributed to Oxford's continuing modest prosperity, even at a time of agricultural depression when rural Oxfordshire was experiencing economic decline and depopulation.

Oxford had no single major industry upon which its fortune depended, and there was indeed a contemporary jest that the city produced 'nothing but parsons and sausages'. In fact, many small industries existed, providing goods and services to both Town and Gown and to the city's growing residential suburbs. In 1901, 880 men and boys were employed in the paper and printing industries, and the University Press was Oxford's largest single employer in 1914, employing around 575 men and more than 200 women and boys. In 1901, 1,303 men worked in domestic service, 609 of them employed in College or Club Service. Transport, building, food, drink and inns, and tailoring were other substantial employers of men, and 662 general labourers were included among the 921 males listed as other workers and dealers. Almost 9,000 of Oxford's 22,800 women and girls over the age of 10 were economically active in 1901, 4,982 of them working in domestic service. A further 1,629 females were employed in tailoring and dress, several hundred at Hyde's and Lucas's large clothing factories in the city centre, but most of them in the home. Lesser numbers of women and girls worked in the professions, especially as teachers, and in occupations focused around food and drink, hotels and lodging-houses. (Appendix Table 2)

Significant local industries included the breweries, Hall's and Morrell's, Salter Bros., boat-builders at Folly Bridge, Lucy's and Dean's iron foundries in Jericho and East East Oxford respectively, and Frank Cooper's Victoria Works in Park End Street, the home of Cooper's Oxford Marmalade from 1903. Beyond the city boundary, in Cowley, the Oxfordshire Steam Ploughing Company had been founded in 1868, and employed 200 people by 1900. In 1909, it was said to be the largest private firm of steamroller and traction-engine owners in the world. In 1912, William Morris, an Oxford cycle and motorcycle maker who had decided to go in for car-making, acquired the former Oxford Military College buildings in Cowley and began production there in March 1913. By the summer of 1914, the business had 86-100 employees and the weekly output of Bullnose Morris cars was close to fifty. Morris was extending the premises with a view to producing around 4,000 cars, including a cheaper Morris Cowley in 1915, and he was about to introduce a smart tradesman's van on the car chassis. Already, the *Oxford Chronicle* noted:

> 'The Morris-Oxford car is quite a feature of the streets of the city, and it is especially popular with the members of the University for it is of convenient size and very easy to drive.'

Still largely confined within its medieval limits in 1801, Oxford spread on every side during the nineteenth century as the city's population grew, creating the 'base and brackish skirt' of suburbs so deplored by the poet Gerard Manley Hopkins. These new developments were particularly evident from Port Meadow and the low hills to the west and south-west of Oxford.

Commentators such as William Tuckwell recalled the first North Oxford villas of the 1860s as 'vaunt-couriers to a tremendous irruption; to the interminable streets of villadom, converging insatiably protuberant upon distant Wolvercot (sic) and Summertown.' Tuckwell also remembered bowling along the Henley road in the 1830s when the towers and spires of Oxford came into view at Rose Hill and could be seen across open fields until you reached The Plain. After Cowley

Field was enclosed in 1853, much of this land was laid out for building, and the area to the south-east of Magdalen Bridge housed nearly thirty per cent of the city's population by 1901. Due to college ownership of potential development land and the topography of Oxford, which limited building on the flood plains of the Thames and Cherwell, the scale of this transformation was less apparent to residents and visitors whose daily lives revolved around the city centre and the railway stations.

During the nineteenth century, increasing numbers of people were deserting the city centre for more spacious houses in the new suburbs. Wealthy tradesmen and professionals, university professors and men and women of independent means set the trend, but they were soon followed by better-paid artisans and craftsmen looking to find 'pretty little cottages, where people might remove from the courts and alleys of the city streets, and dwell in comfort and peace'. After 1877, college fellows were allowed to marry and retain their fellowships, thus creating a new and growing demand for properties in fashionable North Oxford. Even the poorest in society were sometimes able to find cheap houses to rent in distant corners of the suburbs when old properties in the city centre were demolished.

As the population in the city centre declined, many old houses were converted into commercial premises or totally redeveloped as banks, shops, hotels or pubs to meet new business requirements. Notable local retailers which prospered during the late nineteenth and early twentieth centuries included the high class grocery business Grimbly Hughes in Cornmarket Street and stores such as Elliston and Cavell, Webber's, Badcock's, Cooper's and Cape's. The Oxford Co-operative Society was founded in George Street in 1871 and had branches across the city and around 7,000 members by 1914. The diminished number of parishioners and growing traffic congestion helped to seal the fate of St Martin's Church which was demolished in 1896, leaving only the medieval tower, as part of the Carfax Improvement Scheme. The northern corners of Carfax were also set back and replaced by Frank East's store (1896-7), later the Midland Bank, and Lloyd's Bank (1900-3).

Physical change to the Town side of Oxford was matched by dramatic Gown developments. Following a series of internal reforms,

**The Carfax Copper stands guard in the middle of the crossroads, 1907.
The store on the left and Lloyd's Bank on the right show how
commercial buildings were changing the look of the city.**

the University embarked on an unparalleled period of growth and the annual number of freshmen rose from an average of 389 in the 1850s to 905 in the 1900s. Permission for students enrolled in college to live more cheaply in licensed lodging houses helped to make a university education available to a wider, if still overwhelmingly middle class, public. From 1879, women were also admitted to the University, but not as yet to take degrees.

Major new University buildings included the Gothic style University Museum in Parks Road, built for the teaching of the natural sciences between 1855 and 1860, and the Examination Schools (1876-82). The latter occupied much of the site of the former Angel Hotel in High Street and displaced many properties in Merton Street. Many colleges built new ranges and quadrangles to accommodate growing student numbers, and three completely new men's colleges, Keble, Mansfield and Manchester, were established in the later nineteenth century. The first women's colleges, Somerville and Lady Margaret Hall, opened in 1879 and they were soon followed by St Hugh's and St Hilda's.

The University was prominent in the everyday life of the city during term-time. Men and women in academic dress were to be seen everywhere, and sporting undergraduates hurried between colleges and the river, the University Parks or more distant sports grounds. Eights' Week in May, when college crews raced on the Thames, became an important social event as well as a sporting one.

The crowded River Thames during Eights' Week, 1913. The annual bumping races, when each college eight aimed to become Head of the River, were a social as well as a sporting event.

Commemoration, or Commem Week at the end of the summer term included concerts, flower shows and college balls. The Encaenia Ceremony, when honorary degrees were awarded at the Sheldonian Theatre, formed the climax of the week, and a semi-public one, involving a procession of academics from the Vice-Chancellor's college.

The military had a more substantial presence in Oxford following Richard Haldane's Army reforms in 1908 which created Oxford University's Officer Training Corps (OTC) out of the old Rifle Volunteers; by 1914, many young men had passed through formal training courses.

Most Oxford residents were probably more aware of the lighter side

City Police officers and undergraduates link arms during a Commemoration Ball, 1914. This was a rare moment of truce in a city where student pranks regularly attracted the attention of the police.

Communications Company of the Oxford University Officer Training Corps in Holywell, 1912. The Racquet Courts building in the background became the headquarters of the 1/4th Battalion Oxfordshire and Buckinghamshire Light Infantry during the war.

Time for a drink outside the White Hart at Wytham, 1913. Signallers from the Oxford University Officer Training Corps pose with their bikes during an exercise break.

of University life, the college rags which burst out into the streets, the mock funeral processions when undergraduates were sent down, and disruptive stunts at the New Theatre.

By 1914, the heart of Oxford looked much as it does today and electric street lighting had been introduced, in the main streets at least, in the 1890s. Motor buses replaced old-fashioned horse trams in 1914 after William Morris, the up-and-coming motor manufacturer, tired of the long controversy over the introduction of electric trams and ran unlicensed buses in opposition to the horse trams from December 1913. Within weeks the tramway company began to run its own buses, and Morris bowed out of the dispute, satisfied that he had broken the deadlock. The modernization of Oxford was only partial, however, and on market days, the main roads leading into the city were still thronged with livestock being driven to the cattle market in Gloucester Green. Carriers' wagons from local towns and villages clustered around St Mary Magdalen Church or parked in Circus Yard on the fringe of the populous inner-city suburb of St Ebbe's.

From its earliest days, Oxford University had welcomed foreign students and teachers, and Oxford scholars were always aware of

New Daimler bus and old horse tram at the Magdalen Road terminus. Impatient with delays in providing modern public transport in Oxford, William Morris and the local solicitor, Frank Gray, introduced rival motor buses to popular acclaim in December 1913.

developments in universities across Europe. In the nineteenth century German universities and scholarship inspired university reform in Oxford and elsewhere and strong cultural links were forged between Oxford and Germany. The Oriental scholar Friedrich Max Müller (1823-1900), born in Dessau and educated at Leipzig, was appointed Taylorian Professor of Modern European Languages in 1854, and Professor of Comparative Philology in 1868, becoming one of the great figures in the Victorian University. Hermann Georg Fiedler (1862-1945) was appointed Taylorian Professor of German in 1903, and founded the Oxford University German Literary Society in 1909. German Rhodes Scholars, under Cecil Rhodes' scheme for Rhodes Scholarships, studied at Oxford from 1903, and two further German societies, the Anglo-German Society (1908) and the Hanover Club (1911), were launched at the University.

Relations between Oxford and Germany were ironically at their warmest in June 1914 when the majority of those receiving honorary degrees were German. The recipients included the composer, Richard Strauss, who

---

OXFORD UNIVERSITY ANGLO-GERMAN SOCIETY

Links between Oxford University and Germany were strongest in the years leading up to 1914. Cecil Rhodes, a student at Oriel College in the 1870s, included Germany in his scheme for Rhodes scholarships and fifty-six students chosen by Kaiser Wilhelm II came to Oxford between 1903 and 1914. Other German students also attended the University and Oxford men completed their education at highly-regarded German universities.

The Oxford University Anglo-German Society was founded by a German Rhodes Scholar in 1908 to improve relations between the two countries. By June 1909 the society had 370 English and 566 German members and opened an upstairs reading room at 50 Cornmarket Street. Oxford members held regular debates, agreeing by a single vote that the system of privately owned railways was 'lamentable,' and disapproving of women's suffrage by the same margin. In May 1913, they decided that the increase in Germany's armaments was not a threat to peace in Europe, and in February 1914 that 'Germany and England ought to be ABSOLUTE ALLIES in the strictest sense of the phrase'. In March 1914 the Anglo-German Society staged a rugby match in fancy dress against the University's Anglo-French Club, winning 21-0.

The Anglo-German Society moved to new club rooms at 23 George Street in May 1914, and it helped to host a dinner for the German ambassador, Prince Lichnowsky, at the Masonic Buildings in High Street when he came to Oxford to receive an honorary degree on 3 June. At the end of term, Baron Wilhelm von Richthofen, a Rhodes Scholar at Lincoln College – and the Red Baron's cousin – was elected Librarian for Michaelmas 1914, but by then of course Great Britain and Germany were at war and the Society was no more.

German members of Oxford's Anglo-German Society at Magdalen College, 1913. German Rhodes Scholars attended the University from 1903 and helped to forge stronger links between Oxford and Germany.
President and Fellows of St John's College, Oxford

became a Doctor of Music, and Prince Lichnowsky, the German ambassador to Great Britain, who became a Doctor of Civil Law. Professor and Mrs Fiedler entertained Prince Lichnowsky to luncheon in Queen's College Hall and the German Literary Society and the Anglo-German Society hosted a dinner for him at the Masonic Buildings in High Street. In his after dinner speech the Prince said that he regarded 'the German Rhodes Scholars as ambassadors of goodwill between two great peoples who each have mighty parts to play in the future of civilization.' Toasts were drunk to both 'The King' and 'The

Kaiser' in a room which was to become a military hospital ward just two months later.

Liberal Oxford opinion could not imagine war with Germany – in the novel *High Table* the Warden of the fictional St Mary's College argues that the idea 'is untenable by anyone who realises how closely the intelligentsia of the two countries are associated. Scholarship, literature, art, know no frontiers.' Gilbert Murray, Regius Professor of Greek, believed that war between civilized states was obsolete and, as the international crisis deepened, he became a member of the British Neutrality Committee. At the end of July, the editor of the Liberal-supporting *Oxford Chronicle* saw Britain primarily as a peacemaker on good terms with Germany, France and Russia. He judged as remote the circumstances which would justify involvement in 'a general European melée'.

Four days later, the German invasion of neutral Belgium as part of a pre-emptive attack on France provided 'a cast-iron excuse for intervention'. During the afternoon of 4 August, the British ambassador in Berlin asked for assurances that Belgium's neutrality would be respected. Germany rejected the approach and Great Britain declared war at 11pm Greenwich Mean Time.

In Oxford, as elsewhere, there were dramatic repercussions. Academic wrangling about the rights and wrongs of war was largely silenced and Professor Murray's opinions were changed by the German invasion of Belgium. *The Oxford Chronicle* reported:

> 'The appalling struggle of the great nations ... is now a dreadful fact, and we Englishmen have to do our part in it.'

The Oxford Chronicle summarises the first few days of the Great War, August 1914. Oxford was already being transformed and the Mayor's appeal anticipated that many people would soon lose their jobs and need financial support.

Patriotic fervour gripped all classes, and Oxford, a sleepy place during the University's Long Vacation, was suddenly filled with soldiers. Orders for general mobilization were received at Cowley Barracks, the regimental depot for the Oxfordshire and Buckinghamshire Light Infantry (Ox and Bucks), on 4 August, and the first reservists began to arrive there the following morning to be armed and equipped as soldiers. They probably included some of the sixty-three men from the Oxford University Press who had been seen off by the Secretary, Edwin Cannan, on the previous day. Most were despatched to join the 2nd Battalion in Aldershot on the 8th, and, on the same day, the 3rd Battalion was mobilized, equipped and sent off to Portsmouth together with the entire establishment of the depot.

During these early days, men from the Territorial Reserve established as part of Richard Haldane's army reforms in 1908 were also flocking to the headquarters of the 4th Battalion in St Cross Road, and they were accommodated in colleges and other buildings before

Men of the 4th Battalion Oxfordshire and Buckinghamshire Light Infantry bear the regimental colours to Christ Church Cathedral, August 1914.

being sent away for training. Officers and men of the Queen's Own Oxfordshire Hussars, the county's other Territorial unit, were scattered around the country on 4 August, and the one-word telegram 'Mobilize' was sent to each man from the regimental headquarters in Paradise Street. A few men joined up the same night, but most joined their squadrons the following day before gathering at Reading on the 11th. Here, some officers were shocked during dinner at the Caversham Bridge Hotel when Winston Churchill, First Lord of the Admiralty and himself an Oxfordshire Hussar, warned them that they were in for at least two years of war because of Prussia's immense military strength.

In early August, the University's Officer Training Corps contacted past and present members, asking whether, in the event of mobilization, they would accept a commission in the Army. Many applied direct to regiments of the Regular Army, but the University established a

William Matthison's view of the Examination Schools, swiftly converted into a military hospital, the Third Southern General Hospital, during August 1914. Many other buildings had to be requisitioned as the number of wounded soldiers increased.

Nominations Board in 'a dingy little room' at 9 Alfred Street where candidates for commissions were interviewed. Over 2,000 men were seen there by the end of September and queues sometimes stretched back into High Street. Harold Macmillan, then an undergraduate at Balliol, remarked:

> 'The general view was that it would be over by Christmas. Our major anxiety was by hook or crook not to miss it.'

As part of the preparation for mobilization in the event of war, the County of Oxford Territorial Force Association had identified a suitable building, the Examination Schools in High Street, which could be readily converted into a 520-bed hospital. The Vice-Chancellor was apparently unaware of this secret plan, and the Rev Andrew Clark reported that the Clerk of the Schools was 'bundled out of his office,

Young patriot on horseback outside a shop in Queen Street, 1914. Children were soon involved in the war, playing soldiers and nurses and helping with collections for good causes.

without time allowed him to write out the records of two examinations then finished'. Nearby colleges had promised beds and bedding for the emergency hospital and Corpus Christi College was already being asked for its quota on 5 August. Colonel George Ranking of the Royal Army Medical Corps was appointed Administrator of the new Third Southern General Hospital which, quite remarkably, was ready by 16 August when the Bishop of Oxford conducted an opening service.

Anticipating deaths at the hospital, Ranking approached the City Council for burial space. The Cemeteries Committee decided in September that soldiers should be buried in Botley Cemetery free of charge if they were British or Allied soldiers, but for a fee of 12/6 (62½p) per burial 'in the case of alien enemies'.

When war began, H.W.B. Joseph, Fellow of New College, started a diary to record how 'an ordinary citizen was affected by a war of such huge extent, the first in which aircraft, submarines, and great steel navies have been used'. On 6 August, he reported that 'everyone is much more cheerful now that war is declared and they are busy usefully'. Rachael Poole later recalled Oxford in the cloudless days of early August as a 'hurly-burly of enthusiastic unauthorised activity out of which the new order of a vast reorganisation gradually emerged ... Everywhere was bustle; everyone worked; the sun shone, the strains of "Tipperary" echoed in every street'.

More than 100 older men were soon parading for daily drill on Balliol College cricket ground under the command of A.D. Godley, the University's Public Orator. Special constables, including many councillors, were enrolled at the Town Hall and local Boy Scouts mobilized for non-military duties with a central office at Exeter College. An Emergency Committee, including well-known Oxford ladies as well as Town and Gown members, was hurriedly formed to raise funds to deal with the economic distress that was everywhere anticipated. May Cannan was involved in the hasty conversion of one wing of Magdalen College School as a Voluntary Aid Detachment hospital which was ready by 6 August, but this subsequently met with official disapproval and was never used. At the University Museum, a temporary workroom was provided where the wives of members of the University, shop assistants, and the wives of working men produced great quantities of clothing for the war effort. Museum staff and Boy

Scouts packed the finished articles and Girl Guides did their bit by threading needles and helping in a hundred other ways.

A number of Oxford men and women were in Germany or on holiday in Europe when war was declared. J.C. Masterman, when appointed to a lectureship at Christ Church in 1913, had been advised by the Dean, the Rev. T.B. Strong, to spend a year in Germany and prepare himself for a teaching career. He was interned in August 1914, and spent four years at the Ruhleben internment camp in Berlin. Educational classes were among the activities organised at the camp, and the future spymaster gave history lectures to fellow inmates. Mark Kearley, from Magdalen College, was another internee at Ruhleben.

One Corpus man, W.H. Wells, a lecturer at Munich University, was later to be conscripted into the German army because he had acquired Bavarian citizenship rights. Emily Penrose, the Principal of Somerville College, was in Switzerland at the outbreak of war, and had 'an adventurous journey home which included wheeling her luggage on a trolley for a couple of miles'. Holidaymakers in Germany in the summer of 1914 included Hilda Pickard-Cambridge, who was staying at Schwalbach near Koblenz, while waiting for her husband, Arthur, a don at Balliol College. She was effectively trapped in her hotel during August before joining an American family on a tense journey by Dutch steamer down the Rhine to Rotterdam.

Hilda Pickard-Cambridge returned to Balliol in early September to find the college full of prospective recruits and with half of its undergraduates already in the forces or government service. Oxford was filled with restless energy and citizens eager for news gathered outside the public library in St Aldate's where the latest war telegrams were posted. Rachael Poole remarked that this was the high tide of courage and hopefulness, even as the first convoys of wounded soldiers began to arrive from the front.

Chapter Two

Preparations at Home

GREAT BRITAIN HAD A REGULAR ARMY of 247,000 professional soldiers at the outbreak of war, many of them stationed overseas. The 1st Battalion Ox and Bucks, the old 43rd Regiment, for example, was quartered at Ahmednagar in India. With the Army Reserve of old soldiers (145,000), a Special Reserve of trained battalions (63,000) and a Territorial Force (268,000) intended for home defence, the country had about 723,000 men at its disposal.

The British Expeditionary Force which landed in France in August 1914 was initially only 100,000 strong. By contrast, the German conscript army had 4.5 million men and the mobilized French army had 3,781,000. The Kaiser's description of Britain's 'contemptibly small army' probably referred to its size rather than its quality, but the phrase became a powerful weapon in the propaganda war. Great Britain's army of volunteers reached 2.5 million by January 1916, but the demand for ever more soldiers led to the introduction of conscription and the increasing recruitment of women to release men for the front line.

As the reservists and Territorials left for further training and action at the front the priority at home was to recruit more men. Lord Kitchener was appointed Secretary of State for War on 5 August and he quickly outlined plans for a much expanded army based on the regular army system. This New Army was to provide half a million men, but his first appeal on 7 August was for 100,000 recruits. Nationally, there was a huge response with 298,923 enlistments in August and 462,901 in September. In Oxford a recruiting office was opened at Balliol College on 19 August and had enrolled 833 recruits by early September. Colour Sergeant J.L. Surman, a University Press man, became a familiar sight in the city, not least at St Giles's Fair in September, and he personally enrolled well over 2,000 recruits. Henry Taunt, the veteran Oxford photographer, did his best for the cause by publishing a recruiting song.

Every Man a Soldier, a recruiting song by the Oxford photographer, Henry Taunt, which was approved by Field Marshal Lord Roberts. Taunt was a keen patriot, but his photographic outings aroused suspicion in the early days of the war.

Recruiting sergeant encouraging men to join the Army at St Giles's Fair, September 1914. He is probably Colour Sergeant J.L. Surman, a University Press employee on war service.

A readiness to volunteer percolated throughout society and there were no evident class barriers. All the eligible male members of some families enlisted, including the four sons of Councillor William Gray from Pembroke Street, St Clement's, and the father and his six sons in the Salcombe household in Essex Street. Old boys of the Oxford Poor Law School in Cowley seemed as keen to enlist as the alumni of Summer Fields prep school in Summertown.

In the Oxford colleges, younger fellows, undergraduates and servants were equally prepared to place themselves in the firing line. Thomas Case, President of Corpus Christi College, was on holiday in Weymouth in August 1914, and, probably because the excellent postal service kept him in touch with the college, he stayed there, receiving a stream of war-related correspondence. Undergraduates wrote seeking leave of absence from the college. E. Sandford Porter, for example, regretted the inevitable break with Corpus Christi:

> 'The three years I have spent there have been the happiest in my life, and I know that the fourth would have been happier still. But I feel that England needs every man she can get for this great struggle, and I am sure you will understand my motives.'

Anthony Muirhead wrote from the British Expeditionary Force to the President of Magdalen College on 3 October 1914, apologising for his non-appearance: 'I am more than sorry that the war has dislocated my last year at Oxford; it is another instance of the Kaiser's disregard for private interests.'

Reginald Tiddy, Fellow of Trinity College, hated war, but joined up out of a sense of duty despite his asthma and being 'so short-sighted as to be almost helpless without his glasses'. As a lieutenant in the 2/4th Battalion Ox and Bucks, he was killed on 10 August 1916 when a shell fell into trenches near Laventie. In one of his last letters, Tiddy asked Dr Blakiston, President of Trinity, to visit Mrs Randall of 17 Abbey Place, St Ebbe's, who had just lost her third son, presumably a college servant, in the war. Sixteen college servants at Corpus Christi College had joined up by June 1917, and the *Oriel Record* in October 1916 described the college as 'fairly denuded of servants by the war'.

Headington Quarry, a village notorious for poaching and fighting, displayed the same 'impetuous patriotism' seen elsewhere. A school teacher, Mr Golby, went to join the Oxfordshire Hussars in October 1914 and died at the Battle of the Somme. Many old boys of the school in the 2/4th Battalion Ox and Bucks were on the casualty lists in March 1918. Two villagers, Dusty Wright and 'Ferret' Taylor, had been in jail when war broke out and soon volunteered for service. They were later recalled as 'blokes like…that when they was out there fightin'… if they see a German, they'd be after 'im …wouldn't wait to be told…

A patriotic Oxford family, Councillor William Gray with his four sons, all of whom had enlisted in the Army by December 1914. One was killed in the war and the other three were wounded during the Battle of the Somme.

they was that type of feller, and they both went "west"'.

From the first, the Government used propaganda to encourage those who were more reluctant to join the fray. The Parliamentary Recruiting Committee issued a series of leaflets urging men to enlist. As soon as Lord Kitchener's original target of half a million men was reached – by September 1914 – a revised leaflet stressed the need for a second half million. By December, as the number approached a million, a second million was demanded. The new message was that 'It will be time to talk about "enough" when the Kaiser admits he's "had enough."'

Lord Kitchener's famous 'Your Country Needs You' poster was published in September to bring the recruiting message to the widest possible audience. Other recruiting leaflets played on men's fears that children would ask 'Father, why weren't you a soldier too?' and urged women to avoid heaping shame on their husbands and sons by not letting them go. Leaflets like 'The Truth about German Atrocities', 'Scientific Savagery', and 'Cold-Blooded Murder' were calculated to enrage the mildest of men. Arnold Toynbee, Fellow of Balliol, assisted in the preparation of atrocity propaganda, especially over Lord Bryce's Commission of Enquiry into German Atrocities in Belgium. The Bryce report was translated into thirty languages, and had a wide circulation in Great Britain, seeking to bolster public opinion against the 'barbaric Hun'. Lewis Farnell, Rector of Exeter College, publicised a story about the Germans burying prisoners alive which he had heard from Belgian refugees. H.W.B. Joseph, at New College, noted in December 1914 the widely circulated tale, almost certainly untrue, of a Canadian soldier who had been crucified by the Germans.

Peer pressure and women's scorn, real or imagined, also played a part in persuading men to enlist. The American Rhodes Scholar, J.B. Langstaff, who studied at Oxford between 1914 and 1916, noted that 'crusading enthusiasm' was sweeping many of his friends into Kitchener's army. Similar emotions must have been hard to resist in a large workplace like Oxford University Press where 356 men went into the services during the war, and 45 were killed. Here, too, it was reported that when Press men were put on short time in September 1914, unmarried men were told their jobs would be kept if they enlisted; if they did not enlist they would be discharged.

Young men in civilian clothes became very conspicuous, and 'Weeper' Smart in Frederic Manning's classic work, *Her Privates We*, tells comrades that he only joined up because he was ashamed to be seen walking in the streets. In 1915, Hilda Stroud pilloried Banbury men who had failed to enlist as 'cowards that's what I think they are'. Women sometimes offered white feathers to such men, or at least damned them with looks of utter contempt.

Cowley Barracks, briefly empty after the departure of reservists on 8 August, became a recruiting centre for the Ox and Bucks, receiving hundreds of men from across the two counties and despatching 10,537 to various units during the first year of the war. The barracks was overwhelmed and those men who could not be billeted in local houses slept on the grass outside the mess or under hedges across Hollow Way. William McDougall, Fellow of Corpus Christi College, supported the

Ox and Bucks recruits head for the GWR railway station, September 1914. Uniforms ran out at Cowley Barracks, and men were sent off to training camps in their civilian clothes.

decision to provide temporary accommodation for recruits in the college in September 1914:

> 'I was told of men having to sleep out of doors without shelter and of cases of acute rheumatism being taken to the hospital in consequence.'

As many as five doctors at a time medically examined the recruits, who were then sent off in batches to join existing units or the four New Army or service battalions that were raised during September and October.

At first, these new recruits had no uniforms, arms or equipment, and batches marched off to the railway station in civilian clothes. Sometimes other men would join them on route and arrive at the destination with no paperwork. The 5th and 6th service battalions of the Ox and Bucks were raised at Camberley in Surrey, but the 7th and 8th battalions were raised at Cowley and went off to training camp in Wiltshire in October. Bad weather forced them back to Oxford in November and they spent the winter in billets and training around the city. They were issued with blue serge uniforms which made them look like postmen. The Rev Andrew Clark, visiting Oxford in December 1914, noted disapprovingly, 'men of the "skinned-rabbit, snippit-tail-less" blue-coated Kitchener's army' in the streets.

The government soon decided that the Territorials would have to serve overseas, and most of the men agreed to this change in their conditions of service. A reserve regiment of the Queen's Own Oxfordshire Hussars (Oxfordshire Hussars) was formed at the beginning of September incorporating both those who had not volunteered to serve abroad and new recruits. It was quartered at Christ Church and used part of Christ Church Meadow as a training ground. In October, the ever-curious Rev Andrew Clark observed signs at the entrances to the meadow, warning of its partial closure 'for military purposes'.

Since the 4th Battalion Ox and Bucks would also be needed for overseas service, Colonel W.H. Ames began raising a second line

Draft of men from the Queen's Own Oxfordshire Hussars in Christ Church Meadow, January 1915. The Meadow Buildings provided temporary barracks at this time and part of the meadow was used for drill and training.

Territorial battalion, the 2/4th, initially for home defence, on 8 September. An orderly room was set up at Exeter College and around 130 recruits were enrolled and billeted on the first day; by early October the battalion was up to full strength. The men were billeted in colleges until the beginning of the Michaelmas Term in October and then mostly in university lodging houses. Uniforms arrived by Christmas and equipment by the end of January but their absence did not prevent a busy training programme which included daily drills on Port Meadow, trench digging behind battalion headquarters in St Cross Road, and route marches which attained a speed of 4mph through Bagley Wood.

Early experience at the front demonstrated the inadequacy of the British artillery and Lieutenant Colonel A. St J. Hamersley MP was authorised in 1915 to recruit a Heavy Battery for Oxford City and County which would form part of the Royal Garrison Artillery. Recruits had to have experience with horses and were promised five shillings a day. Exeter College was the headquarters for this new battery, the 128th Oxfordshire Heavy Battery, which reached full strength by mid-April. Recruiting for a second battery, the 132nd, began in the same month and the War Office asked Hamersley to raise a third, the 135th, in August. Recruiting for this battery – and for a fourth, the 156th – was at Exeter College or 47 High Street. The headquarters of the 135th had been moved to Brasenose College by October. The 128th Battery initially trained in the University Parks with wooden guns which were parked outside Exeter College chapel when not in use. It later bivouacked with the 132nd at Headington before both moved to Charlton Park at Woolwich for further training.

County units provided the main focus for local recruitment, and there were no Pals battalions in Oxfordshire like those formed in major cities. Units raised in Oxford or Cowley recruited men from the wider area, although A Squadron of the Oxfordshire Hussars at the outbreak of war had been mainly recruited from the city. University men, in particular, might prefer to enlist in regiments nearer to home, but choice of a regiment might depend on having a colleague with an uncle in it or on the appeal of its cap badge. Others volunteered for the Royal Navy which had its own recruiting office in Cowley Road by April 1916.

A soldier's wife and son say goodbye in Queen Street, February 1915. These men from the Oxfordshire Hussars were on their way from Christ Church to the GWR railway station.

The local nature of the new service battalions was diluted from the first by drafts from elsewhere; Alec Gold recalled that his platoon in the 5th Battalion Royal Berkshire Regiment included Brummies and Cockneys as well as Berkshire men. At first the three groups could barely understand each other, a particular hazard when using field telephones! Frank Gray noted that many recruits at Cowley Barracks in February 1917 were from London and Birmingham, and the regional identity of units in the army was further eroded as battalions were merged and new drafts replaced casualties.

Recruitment fell off after the initial rush to the colours and the authorities resorted to various strategies to boost enlistment. Military rallies sought to stir the patriotism of potential recruits, but a parade through Oxford of over 3,000 troops-in-training led by the Oxfordshire Hussars band in January 1915 was said to have attracted middle-aged men, women and girls, not the intended audience. In June, a recruiting march through Oxfordshire and Buckinghamshire by representatives of local regiments culminated in Oxford with a military band playing in St Giles' and a film showing war episodes at the Corn Exchange. The *Oxford Chronicle* reported that 'a number of young men promised to enlist'.

A Great Military Rally was held in Oxford on 2 October which brought 500 men of the Oxfordshire Heavy Batteries from Woolwich with their guns, horses and wagons and included a review of troops in South Park. Later there was a torchlight procession from St Giles' to the Yeomanry headquarters in Paradise Street where over 2,000 people packed into a meeting which ended with a recruiting appeal. Public meetings provided a less dramatic way of encouraging recruitment. At a gathering at the Martyrs' Memorial in October 1915, the Rev A. Goldring criticised the two million eligible men who had still to come forward, and distributed leaflets detailing German atrocities against

Canadians joining the Oxfordshire Hussars near the regimental headquarters in St Thomas's, March 1915. Many Canadians enlisted in their own expeditionary force, and these men were perhaps recent settlers who retained links with the city and county.

FRANK GRAY'S RECRUITMENT

Frank Gray (1880-1935) was the son of Alderman Walter Gray, six times Mayor of Oxford, and a pillar in the local Conservative establishment. Frank became a solicitor in Oxford and came to public notice in 1913-14 when he helped William Morris in the struggle to introduce motor buses. Frank Gray secured exemption from military service on business grounds when conscription was introduced, but he joined up to set an example in February 1917, 'anxious to do exactly as the lowest does.' He recorded his army life in a regular column, 'Confessions of a Private', in the *Oxford Chronicle*, which was published in book form in 1920.

Dropped off by his chauffeur, Gray was soon disenchanted by the recruitment process:

> 'I went to the recruiting office, 90, High Street, Oxford, at 9.30am. I had to wait until after 11, and then, with other recruits, I was taken before the officer in charge; and next, under the care of a sergeant who cycled behind us, we went by bus to the barracks at Cowley. From 11.30 to 1 o'clock we wasted our time in the gymnasium waiting for the completion of certain formalities. From 1 to 2 we went to dinner at the canteen. From 2 to 4 there was more waste of time and more formalities...I went to my barrack-room where I was told to make my bed. Having done it, I was discharged for the day, the remainder of which I spent in gossiping, meeting some very interesting fellows.'

Gray, after his idlest day for eighteen years, was appalled by the 'extraordinary unreadiness' at the barracks, and his experiences in France did nothing to restore his faith in the system. After the war, he became a populist Liberal politician, and MP for Oxford City between 1922 and 1925

women and children and their brutal tyranny towards working men. However, the experiences of A.L. Smith, Master of Balliol from 1916, at WEA classes suggested that young men greeted recruiting drives with the claim that they wouldn't 'be any worse off under German rule'.

Throughout 1915 the introduction of conscription remained a matter of serious debate. Lewis Farnell, Rector of Exeter College, was an eager propagandist for the National Service League, established in 1901 to press for compulsory military service. He was one of the fourteen Oxford Heads of Houses who wrote to *The Times* in June 1915 calling for legislation to set up a national service for the home, workshop and fighting line to replace 'the voluntary go-as-you-please methods'. Eighty members of the University, most of them presumably undergraduates, wrote to the *Daily Chronicle* opposing conscription and they were at once branded as 'foreigners – or "slackers"'.

The National Service Act in 1915 was one consequence of the debate, setting out to register the details of everyone between 15 and 65. This National Register showed, by deducting 'essential' workers, how many men were still available for military service. Lord Derby was appointed in October to give voluntary recruiting a last chance, using the National Register to make a direct appeal to men of military age. Recruiting did increase and the new recruiting office at 90 High Street was besieged as hundreds sought to enlist or attest with the obligation to serve if called upon; around fifty per cent were rejected as medically unfit.

When the Lord Derby scheme ended in December 1915, it was calculated that some 600,000 men had still evaded enrolment and conscription was introduced as a 'necessary evil' through Military Service Acts passed in 1916. The editor of the *Oxford Chronicle* defended the voluntary system to the end, arguing that it had served the country well, and he warned that many of the men brought in by conscription would prove to be physically unfit. Conscription for single men aged between 18 and 41 began in March 1916, and it was extended to married men in May. Local tribunals were established to hear appeals for exemption on the grounds of indispensable work, serious hardship, ill-health or infirmity, and conscientious objection. Inevitably, it was the conscientious objectors who attracted most attention when the Oxford Local Tribunal hearings began. Public opinion was generally hostile and an anonymous correspondent to the *Oxford Chronicle* accused the press of viewing them as people 'with a sort of jelly-fish constitution'.

Socialists at the University accounted for some of Oxford's conscientious objectors. The University's Socialist Society had around 125 members in 1914 and decided in early 1915 not to express an opinion about the war. Many members joined the rush to enlist, but a few chose not to do so. Oxford also had theological students in training for the ministry who were at first exempt from military service. The American, J.B. Langstaff, criticised a fellow undergraduate, Dick Graham, in 1915: '[he] has a "Quaker bug" of not fighting but makes everyone feel like punching his head for the things he does and says'.

In March 1916, Langstaff attended a tribunal hearing which featured several university acquaintances. One theological student wrong-footed the military representative by completing the Biblical 'eye for an eye' quotation to show that it supported peaceful co-existence. Joseph Kaye, a St John's College undergraduate, refused at this hearing to assist in 'the organised murder of fellow men and fellow socialists'. He was later imprisoned for two months for circulating anti-conscription leaflets but was freed on bail after an appeal. In November, he secured conditional exemption from service while working under Sidney Webb as acting secretary at the Fabian Research Department. Another Socialist, Rajani Dutt, a Balliol student, was exempted from combatant service in 1916, and failed on appeal to secure complete exemption. He was imprisoned and sent down from the University for distributing socialist anti-war propaganda in 1917.

Raymond Postgate, another St John's man, a pacifist and chairman of the Socialist Society, was sent to prison in April 1916 after refusing to pay a fine imposed for failing to report for military service. After he was released he was taken to Cowley Barracks where he declined to co-operate and slept naked rather than wear 'the hated livery of militarism. Even army blankets were, in his eyes, connected with the degradation of uniform, and were cast aside'. His case was resolved when a doctor found him physically unfit for military service and he joined the Friends' Ambulance Service. G.D.H. Cole, Fellow of Magdalen College, secured exemption as an unpaid research officer for the Amalgamated Society of Engineers, work judged to be of national importance because it was connected with the munitions industry.

The Oxford tribunal, like others, generally chose to exempt conscientious objectors only from military service and they were therefore required to perform approved non-combatant work. In June 1916, for example, Robert Godley, a City Council road sweeper, was ordered to find work of national importance within three weeks, and William Hine, an Oxford tailor and a member of the Plymouth Brethren, was given the same ultimatum in July.

The bulk of the Oxford Local Tribunal's workload involved trying to weigh the relentless manpower demands of the military against civilian work which might also be contributing to the war effort. Small businesses were a particularly difficult area, since calling up one man could destroy them.

In April 1916, Pearson's ironmongery business at 21-23 George Street announced that it was closing down because the proprietor, Arthur Pearson, had been called up. In October, Basil Blackwell secured conditional exemption on business grounds as a one-man publisher, quite separate from his father's bookshop in Broad Street.

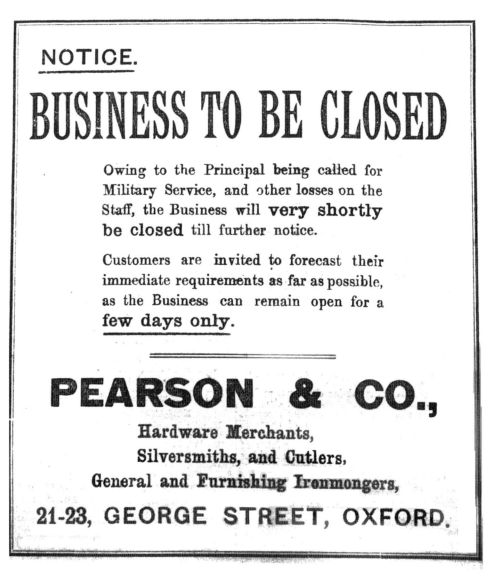

Pearson & Co, ironmongers in George Street, give notice of imminent closure, April 1916. In a typical case, the Oxford Local Tribunal had decided that the military's need for manpower was more important than keeping Arthur Pearson's business open.

One case in May 1917 involved Harry Best, a civil engineer and sanitary surveyor, who had been preparing plans and specifications for work in Oxford military hospitals since the outbreak of war. His exemption was refused despite the evidence of Colonel Ames, Secretary of the Oxfordshire Territorial Force Association, and the view of Colonel Ranking, Administrator of the Third Southern General Hospital, that 'it would be madness' to dispense with a man with his expertise.

Other cases concerned college servants who were catering for the military billeted in colleges. In June 1916, for example, two waiters at St John's College were given temporary exemption after the Junior Bursar countered the evidence of Captain Fox, the military representative on the tribunal, with Colonel Stenning's opinion that the men should be retained.

Proving ill health and infirmity became increasingly difficult as medical boards came under pressure to fill the ranks, and passed as fit, at least for home service, men who had previously been rejected. In an extreme case at Cowley Barracks an officer noted that a new recruit in a batch from Birmingham looked very lame and discovered that he had only one leg. When asked if he'd been medically examined, the man said, 'Yes, but all they did was look at my tongue!'

The Manpower Act in 1918 raised the conscription age from 41 to 50, threatening to empty Oxford of its older dons and college servants. H.W.B. Joseph, Fellow of New College, was graded B2 at a medical examination at Holywell Music Room in July, and he was then conducted to the recruiting office at 90 High Street to collect his grading paper and the sum of 3/6d (17½p). He took the money because he doubted whether the machinery existed for the Government to keep it.

Lieutenant Charles Carrington of the Warwickshire Regiment claimed that the Army could transform 'weedy, sallow, skinny, frightened children – the refuse of our industrial system' into 'handsome, ruddy, upstanding, square-shouldered young men' after six months of good food, fresh air and physical exercise. This was clearly not true of members of the Agricultural Companies formed in 1917 from men who were deemed surplus to the immediate requirements of the army and munitions work. Three of these companies, the 396th,

Queen Mary's Women's Army Auxiliary Corps outside the Sheldonian Theatre, July 1918. The parade and inspection by Lieutenant General Sir Henry Sclater were part of a recruiting campaign, aiming to enlist another 30,000 women and release more men for front line service.

the 574th, and the 646th, were based at Cowley Barracks by May 1918, with a total of around 2,700 men. Medical boards visited the barracks in July to 'comb-out' fit men for front line service, but 2,500 men were still there in the three companies at the end of the war.

Women replaced men in many areas of work during the war, and they were soon employed in the services. A Women's Legion of cooks and drivers was formed in 1914 and this was re-founded as the

Women's Army Auxiliary Corps, an official auxiliary to the armed forces, in March 1917. A public meeting was held at the Oxford Union Society Debating Hall in December as part of a national appeal for 200,000 women soldiers who would be able to release men for fighting duties. These women served as drivers, mechanics, clerks, cooks, storekeepers and typists, some of them close to the front line. The Corps was renamed Queen Mary's Auxiliary Army Corps in 1918 because of the gallantry of its members during the German offensive in March.

The Women's Royal Naval Service was founded in 1917 and Aline Thornton was working as a despatch rider for the Royal Flying Corps (RFC) by June 1917, presumably at the Port Meadow aerodrome, when she was fined for speeding at between 30 and 40 mph in Woodstock Road. She was riding a motorcycle and sidecar with a woman passenger and hurrying to get on duty. When stopped by the police, she commented: 'I can do 48 miles an hour on this machine'. In the same month, Miss Houghton, a driver with the RFC, knocked down a taxi-driver in Broad Street while driving two captains stationed at Christ Church. The Women's Royal Air Force (WRAF) was formed in April 1918 when the RFC merged with the Royal Naval Air Service to form the Royal Air Force. At the end of the war, Grace Hallam was working locally as a WRAF telephonist, and knew about the armistice two days early. Unable to divulge this secret information, she sent her mother a telegram: 'Old Tom will strike 11th of November, 11am'.

Chapter Three

Work of War

THE OUTBREAK OF WAR was widely expected to have serious economic consequences and disruption at Oxford seemed inevitable. The hollowing out of the University, the chief source of the city's prosperity, promised ruin for lodging-house keepers and reduced custom for local businesses. The University and Colleges faced the daunting prospect of reduced tuition and examination fees and diminished rental income from local property. Local firms and corporations lost substantial numbers of their employees and supplies could no longer be guaranteed. In the face of these challenges, a different wartime Oxford soon emerged as College, University, and other public buildings filled with billeted troops and wounded soldiers. College fellows, both male and female, undertook vital war work, and women generally found employment in a host of new areas. Local businesses adapted by making munitions, supplying other military requirements, or simply taking advantage of war conditions.

The plight of Oxford's lodging-house keepers was a prominent concern in the early months of the war. In the Easter Term 1914, the University Delegacy of Lodging-Houses had 955 undergraduates living in 394 licensed lodging-houses, mostly in central and north Oxford and in more select East Oxford roads. Most of the lodging-house keepers were women, eking out a living by themselves or supplementing the household income. War broke out during the Long Vacation, and only 319 of the undergraduates who had agreed to take rooms arrived for the Michaelmas Term in October. J.R.R. Tolkien of Exeter College was one of them, living in lodgings at 59 St John Street and completing his degree in English Language and Literature before taking a commission in 1915. The Delegacy sympathised with lodging-house keepers over their loss of income, and resolved that undergraduates who had enlisted should be asked to pay as compensation one term's rent with a deduction for unused fuel and light. J.A. Carter, now with the Duke of

Cornwall's Light Infantry, replied to his landlady, Miss Penstone of 5 Iffley Road in September 1914: 'I am sorry to be leaving you in the lurch, but after all the expenses I have incurred of uniform and equipment, I simply have not got the money to pay a term's rent in advance.' In these circumstance, G.B. Cronshaw, Bursar of Queen's College, paid off his debt.

The lodging-house keepers were clearly grateful for the Delegacy's support, and G. Milward of 29 Walton Crescent wrote to the Controller in November, acknowledging receipt of half a term's rent sent by the mother of another undergraduate, F.H.F Booth: 'I am very thankful to her for sending it and to you for telling me to write to her. I have two soldiers witch is all I could take untill term is out.'(sic)

Taking in soldiers was a lifeline for some licensed lodging-house keepers and for the owners of other properties that the Delegacy of Lodging-Houses would have deemed unsuitable. A.D. Godley reported to the city's War Executive Committee in December 1914 that use by soldiers had recouped the losses of 83 of the 187 licensed lodging-houses hardest hit by the war. The Delegacy monitored the military use of lodging-houses for a time, noting, for example, that Mrs Flower at 14 Beaumont Street 'has 12 Territorials 5.10.14 - only kept them a few weeks - 8.2.15'.

In November 1914, the 7th and 8th Service Battalions Ox and Bucks were billeted in Oxford after suffering abysmal weather at their training camp in Codford, Wiltshire. The 7th Battalion was billeted in houses to the north of the city centre and in Jericho with its headquarters in Wellington Square. The 8th Battalion was housed in East Oxford as far out as Bullingdon Road with its headquarters at Wesley Hall in Jeune Street. Householders provided mattresses or straw palliasses, not beds, and breakfast, dinner and tea for each man for 2/6d (12½p) a day. The two battalions over-wintered in Oxford before leaving for further training in April 1915. In east Oxford, the men of the 8th Battalion had earned a reputation as excellent family men, cleaning windows, helping in the house, digging gardens, and in many cases taking the place of sons at the front.

There were fears that this might be the end of large-scale billeting in private houses, but, following an appeal from the Town Clerk, the War Office sent some 3,500 men to Oxford in the winter of 1915, including drafts of the 3/4th Battalion Ox and Bucks, the Army Service Corps and the Royal Fusiliers. J.N. Dykes, training with the 29th Royal Fusiliers, was billeted with the Martin family at 9 Juxon Street and enjoyed being mothered by Mrs Martin and hero-worshipped by her young son. He also had fond memories of sitting on the sofa in front of the fire with Margery Wright, a family friend, on his knee! One critic complained that billetees were not being placed in the areas most in need of the money but were housed in Summertown, South Oxford, and in East Oxford out to Magdalen Road, far beyond the Lodging-House Delegacy limits.

Oxford colleges, facing a financial crisis of their own, could display both patriotism and sagacity by agreeing to accommodate the military. Many colleges housed recruits in the early weeks of the war, and on 4 August, H.W.B Joseph was asked to find room for 120 Territorials at New College for five nights until they could move to Cowley Barracks. They occupied three lecture rooms and the North Common Room in Robinson Tower and the college provided mattresses, and use of the

Non-commissioned officers of the 27th Battalion Royal Fusiliers outside Wesley Hall, their Jeune Street headquarters, March 1916. Men from the 27th Battalion were billeted in east Oxford homes during the winter of 1915-16 while completing their training.

hall, latrines and washing facilities. In September, the college agreed to provide board and lodgings for officers of the 4th Battalion Ox and Bucks for 5/- (25p) a day, excluding drinks and smokes. Very much aware of the college's looming annual deficit of around £5,100, Joseph noted that the Oxfordshire Yeomanry stationed at Christ Church were being charged, or were at least paying, 5/- a day for messing alone.

During 1914 and 1915, Exeter College was home to Officers' Training Corps signallers, the headquarters of the 2/4th Battalion Ox and Bucks and three heavy batteries. Oxford's military training role in wartime was formalized in January 1915 when the War Office sent the first batch of 200 newly-commissioned officers to attend a training course organised by the University's Officers' Training Corps. These men were accommodated at Balliol, Hertford, Keble, Trinity, Wadham and Worcester Colleges. By the time Exeter College was added to this list in Michaelmas Term 1915, 400 men were attending each six week course and about 3,000 officers had been trained by March 1916.

The War Office then introduced a new course of officer training, lasting initially for four months and later for seven. Officer Cadet Battalions (OCBs), each consisting of around 750 men, were formed to train serving non-commissioned officers and men for commissions in the army. Two of these units were stationed in Oxford, the 4th with its headquarters at Keble, and the 6th based at Balliol. Companies were also housed at Hertford, New College, Magdalen, St John's College, Wadham and Worcester. F.F. Urquhart recalled 'a comparatively mild military invasion' of Balliol College before March 1916. Subsequently, with many more cadets, the college became more like a barracks and the quadrangle resembled a drill square. A bugle and drums began the day and gentle explosions accompanied gas drills. The cadets had lectures at the Oxford Union and trained in the hills around the city, but they still had time for inter-college sport and became virtual members of the University before returning to the war. The OCBs, about twenty-five per cent of whom were Australians, New Zealanders or Canadians, became a lively part of Oxford life until December 1918.

A School of Aeronautics was established at Oxford in 1915, initially to train young officers and later to train about 1,000 cadets. The school took over the University Museum and some science departments for teaching purposes. Royal Flying Corps cadets and mechanics were

Members of the 6th Officer Cadet Battalion from Balliol College take a break outside St Lawrence's Church in North Hinksey, 1917. Drafts of officer cadets occupied most of Oxford's men's colleges from 1916, attending lectures and undergoing practical military training.
Master and Fellows of Balliol College, Oxford

quartered at eight colleges, Christ Church, Brasenose, Corpus Christi, Exeter, Jesus, Lincoln, Pembroke, and Queen's, and a tented camp was built in the University Parks. An aerodrome was being built on Port Meadow in June 1916 and the first planes arrived in August. The airfield was a temporary facility, intended only for use during the war, with hangars of the Bessonneau type, and tented accommodation. A number of training squadrons subsequently used Port Meadow and No. 2 School of Wireless Training might have been based here from autumn 1916. The skies around Oxford buzzed with aircraft, as Margot Collinson, an undergraduate at St Hilda's College, and her friend, Bronwen, discovered when they went for a walk up Woodstock Road in February 1918. While they sat on a wall and ate their lunch 'several aeroplanes performed for our benefit. We saw one come to earth, and it did bump as it touched the ground. I had never actually seen one land before.'

There were regular accidents and fatalities included Lieutenant J.R. Nickson, a Canadian pilot, and his American observer, Lieutenant William Bly, whose Bristol plane stalled and crashed at Wytham in January 1918. Bly was probably one of the 150 United States Army trainee pilots who had arrived in Oxford in October 1917 and were

Convalescent German prisoners of war are marched along High Street under military escort, October 1914. Wounded German soldiers were among the first patients at the Third Southern General Hospital, and these men were off to a POW camp near Newbury.

stationed at Christ Church and Queen's College. One man described Christ Church as 'our barracks' and said it must be 'a million years old: I know, because it took it that long to cool off to this temperature'.

The swift transformation of the Examination Schools into the Base Hospital for the Third Southern General Hospital was only the first stage of a process which saw many Oxford buildings taken over as war casualties mounted. The Non-Collegiate Delegacy building next to the Exam Schools and the recently built Masonic Buildings opposite were requisitioned immediately, and by 18 August Colonel Ranking was being asked to provide twice as many beds. New College was readily accessible at the rear of the Masonic Buildings and his first thought was to erect hospital marquees in the garden and house nurses and orderlies in the college buildings. The governing

body feared that this might mean suppressing the college and offered only the garden.

The first trainload of around 150 wounded soldiers arrived in Oxford during the afternoon of Sunday, 13 September and people gathered outside the Examination Schools to welcome them. Cheers greeted the Allied wounded, but about forty Germans in their grey uniforms 'passed into the Schools in complete silence and, it may be added, without any demonstration of hostility'. Rumours of misbehaviour by the German patients were stoutly denied, and one visitor reported that they 'seem friendly and genial beings, almost touchingly appreciative of any kindness'. As the Germans recovered they were transferred to a prisoner of war camp near Newbury, and Oxford hospitals subsequently received only Allied wounded until late in the war.

Convalescing soldiers were able to stroll in New College garden from the first, and a tented hospital was erected there in November, eventually occupying the whole area beyond the Mound. By the end of October, 100 beds were being provided in the Town Hall, with the

Nurses and wounded soldiers in New College garden, about 1916. A tented hospital was established in the college garden in November 1914 as the increasing number of casualties forced the Third Southern General Hospital to find extra space.

prospect of more in the Assembly Room and the Drill Hall.

Somerville College, conveniently located next to the Radcliffe Infirmary, attracted Colonel Ranking's attention at the end of March 1915. After rapid three-way negotiations between the War Office, Somerville and Oriel College, Somerville migrated to Oriel's St Mary Hall quad in May, and, in the words of the Principal, Emily Penrose, 'gladly surrendered their College and Garden for the use of the wounded'. Somerville opened as a military hospital at the end of May and Vera Brittain remarked: 'It is really splendid – much better as a Hospital than as a College.'

Three nurses outside the Library Wing at the Somerville Section of the Third Southern General Hospital, September 1918. Somerville College was conveniently placed next to the Radcliffe Infirmary and it became an officers' hospital after the military took it over in April 1915.
Somerville College, University of Oxford

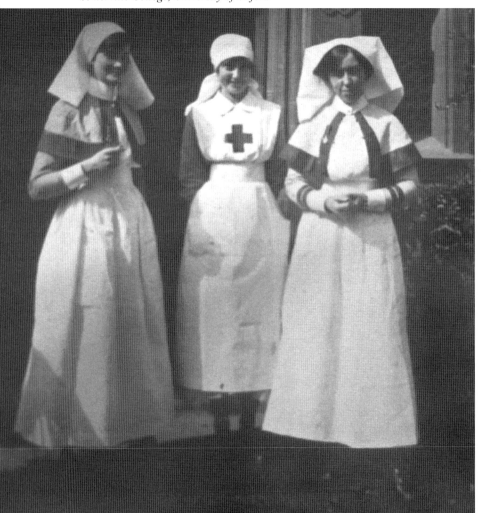

The almost new Maitland Building was reserved for officers from the beginning, and, from 1916, the whole hospital was designated for officers only. Distinguished occupants included Siegfried Sassoon, recovering from gastric fever, who thought the place 'very much like paradise', and Robert Graves, who drifted down to the Cadena café in Cornmarket for coffee in his dressing gown and pyjamas. In October 1915, the Board of Guardians was told that Oxford Workhouse in Cowley Road must be handed over to the War Office as soon as possible. The inmates were transferred to other local workhouses and the building was refitted with an operating theatre, lifts and electricity before the first wounded soldiers were sent there in June 1916. Meanwhile, the Base Hospital in the Examination Schools had expanded westwards into University College's Durham Buildings early in 1916, and it took over Radcliffe Quad and the east side of Front Quad in March 1917. As hospital staffing numbers rose, 170 nurses from the Base Hospital occupied Merton College's St Alban Hall Quad, probably in 1916.

From the beginning the Radcliffe Infirmary was closely associated with the Third Southern General Hospital. Its senior doctors were given commissions in the Royal Army Medical Corps and took charge of wards at the Examination Schools. Dr Collier never adapted to the wearing of uniform, raising his military cap to ladies in the street, and he once scandalised the duty sergeant by wearing his uniform with a bowler hat! The Radcliffe Infirmary had a sixty-bed ward for wounded soldiers, and the nearby Oxford Eye Hospital also received many in- and out-patient cases.

Oxford became a great medical centre during the war, and not only in quantitative terms. The Third Southern General Hospital initially had around 500 beds, and ended the war with getting on for 3,000 at the Base Hospital and its many subsidiaries. The St John's Ambulance Brigade's Oxford Corps conveyed more than 105,000 casualties from the GWR railway station to the Oxford hospitals during the war. Treatment too had been much improved, and, in some areas, revolutionised. Captain Gathorne Girdlestone undertook pioneering orthopaedic work at the Base Hospital and he attended patients at the Voluntary Aid Detachment (VAD) hospital, a convalescent orthopaedic hospital which opened at Felstead House in Banbury Road in May

Boot repairing workshop for soldiers recuperating at the Cowley Road section of the Third Southern General Hospital, about 1916. There were also carpentry workshops, and bed-ridden patients were encouraged to occupy their time sewing regimental crests and other fancy needlework.

Beds and patients fill the auditorium and balconies at the Town Hall, about 1916. The Town Hall became part of the Third Southern General Hospital in November 1914 and beds later occupied both the Assembly Room and the Drill Hall.

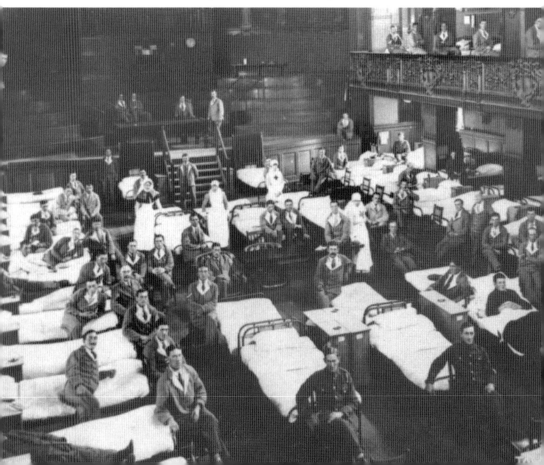

Physiotherapy room at the Third Southern General Hospital, about 1916. The military hospital became a significant orthopaedic centre through the work of Captain Gathorne Girdlestone, using massage and exercise to rehabilitate many injured soldiers.

1915. The Wingfield Convalescent Home in Headington was offered to the War Office at the outbreak of war, and it too became an auxiliary hospital attached to the Base Hospital. In 1917, the Inspector of Military Orthopaedics recommended setting up an Oxford Orthopaedic Centre headed by Girdlestone, and the Wingfield was much extended to provide a 600-bed hospital, a nurses' home and workshops both for rehabilitation and for making appliances.

Shell-shock was gradually recognised as a medical condition during the war, and fascinated the Oxford psychologist, William McDougall, Wilde Reader in Mental Philosophy, who was treating patients with many different symptoms at the Base Hospital by 1917. One of his patients, recovering in the tented hospital in New College garden, had an unfortunate relapse after part of the old city wall suddenly collapsed near his bed. Specialist hospitals were needed for the growing number of sufferers from shell-shock, and the Army Council considered taking over Lady Margaret Hall, ruling it out perhaps because 'the incessant drilling and bugling in the Parks would have made it most unsuitable'. Littlemore Asylum was chosen instead in 1918, and re-opened as the Ashhurst War Hospital in September with a first batch of 100 patients after a complete re-fit.

Academic life virtually ceased to exist in men's colleges and many dons undertook a huge variety of war work. In 1913/14, about 3,000 male undergraduates and around 100 postgraduates attended the University. By 1915, there was less than a third of the pre-war population, and the proportion fell to eighteen per cent in 1916, fifteen per cent in 1917, and just twelve per cent in 1918. At Trinity College, the number of undergraduates fell from 150 in 1914 to 14 in 1917, at Exeter from about 50 to 7, and at Oriel from 133 to 10. At University College, the few remaining dons and undergraduates were described in 1916/17 as 'an exiguous remnant'. At Magdalen, J.B. Langstaff noted 'the bewilderment and concern with which the dons were contemplating their college now that practically the whole student body had been snatched away from under them'.

For the next four years the few male undergraduates were mostly foreigners, young men below military age, men who were medically unfit for service, and men invalided out of the services. The American, T.S. Eliot, for example, studied at Merton during the first year of the war. C.S. Lewis was at University College in 1917 before taking a commission and returned to finish his degree after the war. Aldous Huxley was exempted because of poor eyesight and got a First at Balliol in 1916. Rhodes Scholars continued to be elected, but the German scholarships were discontinued in 1916 and reallocated to Allied countries.

Scientists in the physiology, chemistry, physics, and pathology laboratories were of obvious importance to the war effort, and the physiologist, J.S. Haldane, for instance, carried out crucial experiments after the Germans' first use of chlorine gas which led to the introduction of the box respirator. Georges Dreyer, Professor of Pathology, was able to convince the military authorities that enteric fever was paratyphoid, not typhoid, and soldiers were subsequently inoculated against it, saving many lives. Bertram Lambert, Fellow of Merton and a chemistry

A diminished band of undergraduates at University College in 1917. C.S. Lewis, top right, was an Irishman who joined up after a year at Oxford, returning after the war to complete his degree.
Master and Fellows of University College, Oxford

lecturer, devised a carbon filter for gas masks. The physiologist and Fellow of Magdalen, Horace Vernon, investigated the health of munitions workers in 1915 and his report led to improvements in their working conditions. Andrea Angel, a lecturer at Christ Church, became chief chemist at the Silvertown munitions factory which was purifying

Andrea Angel, a Christ Church don who became chief chemist at the Silvertown munitions factory in East London. He was killed in a devastating explosion while trying to extinguish a fire at the plant on 19 January 1917.

TNT in a populous area of East London. He died while trying to extinguish a fire at the plant on 19 January 1917 when a devastating explosion killed 73 people, injured another 400, and demolished 3,000 houses.

John Townsend, Professor of Physics, undertook wireless research for the Royal Navy. The expertise of other academics proved useful in unexpected ways. G.B. Grundy, Fellow of Corpus Christi College, was a historian with an intimate knowledge of northern Greece and Macedonia. He spent a year at the War Office, working on a route-book for the area, and later advised Naval Intelligence at the Admiralty about small bays and inlets on the Greek coast where U-boats might lurk. H.W.B. Joseph, from New College, also undertook temporary Intelligence work, gleaning information about the river Danube from German books, 'part pilot, part Baedeker'. David Hogarth, Fellow of Magdalen and Keeper of the Ashmolean Museum, possessed vital information about the Arab world and the Ottoman Empire following his archaeological excavations in the Near East. From March 1916, he was based in Cairo with the Arab Bureau and helped to launch the Arab uprising in which his archaeological disciple, T.E. Lawrence, was to play a major role. Unlike many dons of military age who enlisted and saw action at the Front, Henry Tizard, an Oriel College don, was plucked from mundane training duties with the Royal Garrison Artillery and became an experimental equipment officer and a test pilot with the Royal Flying Corps.

The women's colleges helped to maintain educational continuity at the University, but many dons and students chose to become involved with the war effort. The number of women students held steady, and St Hugh's College, which moved into fine new buildings in 1916, was already full by the end of 1917 with ten students living in rooms outside the college. Women became much more integrated within the University and Margaret Verini, an undergraduate at St Hilda's College, recalled that 'older male coaches hadn't any pupils, so some took on women for the first time – both at lectures and tutorials – to earn money'. A new Bachelor of Medicine degree provided new opportunities for women students in 1917. Nevertheless, old dons criticised Oriel College for welcoming the migration of Somerville College in 1915, and C.R.L. Fletcher commented acidly that 'the young ladies, instead of going to be trained as nurses, determine to pursue their ordinary "studies" (and their games) in Oxford'. This was indeed the great dilemma for University women, and Vera Brittain, studying at Somerville in the first year of the war while her fiancé was in the trenches, decided to leave and train as a VAD nurse in June 1915.

Some female dons took leave of absence for long periods. Dr D.C. Maude, from Somerville College, treated wounded Belgians in 1914-15, served in Serbia as an assistant surgeon and anaesthetist in 1915, and then worked for the Wounded Allies Relief Fund in Salonika in 1916-17. Misses Fry and Pope, also from Somerville, shared the administrative work of the Friends' War Victims Relief Expedition in devastated areas of north-east France in 1915 and 1916. Miss Lorimer worked for the Admiralty in London for part of 1916, later edited the *Basra Times*, and had a spell working as an orderly at the Scottish Women's Hospital in Salonika before returning to England in October 1917. At Lady Margaret Hall, Grace Hadow resigned as a lecturer to become Assistant Director of Welfare in the Ministry of Munitions in 1917, and the Vice-Principal, Eleanor Lodge, took leave of absence in Trinity Term 1918 to direct Oxford Women's Canteens for French soldiers close to the front line in France.

Oxford firms found new markets, or changed their products to meet wartime conditions. Oxford University Press was immediately called upon to print, *Why We Are at War: the British Case*, written by members of the Oxford History School and published on 14 September 1914. The book was translated – in Oxford – into six languages, including German, and it led to the publication of a series of eighty-seven Oxford pamphlets on the war by September 1915. These included C.R.L. Fletcher's *The Germans, Their Empire and What They Covet*, and Sir Walter Raleigh's *Might is Right* which even he admitted was 'a fish-wife's tirade on Germany'. The demand for Bibles reached a new peak, and over a million copies of the New Testament were supplied each year for 'use in the field'. The output of learned books was much reduced, but the Press was kept busy printing secret documents for the Admiralty.

At Cowley, the Oxfordshire Steam Ploughing Company had nineteen sets of steam ploughs working across the country during the war and John Allen, the managing director, was awarded the OBE for his work as Honorary Adviser to the Food Production Department which brought many thousands of acres of land into cultivation. Allen and William Morris were key members of the local munitions board established by the Government in 1915 as part of its drive to increase shell production. The Oxfordshire Steam Ploughing Company agreed to manufacture 200 Stokes mortar bombs a week, rising to 1,000 or more. Morris's war-time business, W.R.M. Ltd secured a contract to produce hand grenades early in 1915 and began to manufacture shells in November. Shell production increased, with Allen's technical help, from 500 a week to at least 3,000 a week in August 1916, and 3,720 a week by January 1917. Later in the war, the firm also produced Stokes mortar bombs and mine-sinkers for sea mines, and a light railway was laid from the works in Hollow Way to the GWR Thame branch line in 1917 to cope with the increased output. The business became the Trench Warfare Factory with Morris as Controller; he was appointed OBE in 1917, his first public honour.

Lucy's iron foundry in Jericho was also manufacturing shells and Stokes mortar bombs, and Barlow & Alden's, incorporating Gill's the ironmongers, made aeroplane engines and sheet metal parts for the War

Armstead's Broad Street shop promotes enjoyable commuting by Swift bicycle, April 1916. Buses in wartime were an unreliable alternative, since the military had requisitioned twelve vehicles in October 1914 and services were hit by manpower and fuel shortages.

Office. The motor engineers, Coxeter's, were making nose-pieces for 4.7 shells in 1916, and Hill, Upton & Co., made high explosive shells as well as installing electric light and machinery in factories, military hospitals and colleges. Salter Bros., built small craft and fast hydroplanes for the Royal Navy, and coach builders, Collins & Sons, supplied the army with wagons made of interchangeable parts. Minty's supplied shell slings for the Ministry of Munitions, and F.R. Barry, serving as an army chaplain, noticed an tent labelled '1915, Minty, Oxford' at his camp in Egypt.

Oxford's clothing factories, Hyde's and Lucas's, secured government contracts to supply clothing for the army, and leather workers, Quelch & Son and James Ray, provided military leggings and Sam Browne belts. Frank Cooper supplied preserves to the services, and eighty-one per cent of Osney Mill's output of flour was said to be for the military in 1917. Many local firms – for example, the bakers, Weeks & Co., Bennett's laundry in St Ebbe's, Anniss & Son, surgical equipment makers, and Wenborn's the cutlers – supplied the essential everyday needs of Oxford's military hospitals and establishments. Tailors such as Castell's, Woodward's and Walter's shared the work of making uniforms for the Officer Cadet Battalions stationed in Oxford. Walters & Co had eleven per cent of the trade and employed twenty-three tailors in April 1917, all but five of whom worked on the Turl Street premises. Walters also claimed an extensive trade with officers, many serving abroad.

Stores continued to do good business in wartime – William Baker's opened a new 'super-shop' on the corner of Broad Street in 1916 and Webber's extended their showrooms in 1917 – and cafés flourished, not least because of the growing popularity of afternoon tea. The war also brought new retail opportunities, for war-related toys, for gifts for men in the services and prisoners of war, and, sadly, for remembrance cards and mourning clothes.

Women in and around Oxford had an increasing range of job opportunities. As young men disappeared from shops, schools, and banks – areas in which women already had a foothold, they were quickly replaced by women and girls. The grocery firm, Grimbly, Hughes had lost over sixty men to the war by August 1917, and was then employing thirty-six females. Cape's the drapers had only four

Women workers, wearing triangular munitions pin badges, at W.R.M. Motors Ltd., in Cowley about 1916. Shell production at the factory began in November 1915, and had risen to over 3,000 a week by early January 1917, when William Morris was employing thirty-three women.

Women ticket collectors at Oxford's Great Western Railway station, June 1915. Transport was badly hit by labour shortages as men joined up and women found wartime employment opportunities as inspectors, bus conductors and delivery drivers.

male employees by October 1917 and fifty-three females. Home & Colonial, a national chain with a branch in Queen Street, had an entirely male workforce before the war, but was employing 1,400 women by August 1916. At Cowley St John Boys' School, the headmaster, Herbert Tozer, saw his last male teacher leave in January 1916 and reported that 'the entire assistant staff now consists of lady teachers'. In May 1917, he gratefully, but with a touch of envy, thanked the head of SS Mary and John School for lending him one of 'his numerous assistant masters' to enable the boys to go swimming. Three 'lady clerks' and youths had taken the place of men at the Oxford Electricity Co Ltd by March 1916, and fifteen female clerks were working at Gillett's Bank in Cornmarket in August 1917.

Women also began to be substituted for men on the railways and on buses. Women ticket inspectors were first noted at Oxford's GWR station in May 1915, and 'girl conductors' made an appearance on the Iffley Road bus route in November. W.R.M. Ltd were employing thirty-three girls at Cowley in January 1917, and the Rev George Moore, vicar of Cowley, strongly objected to the sight of 'girls smoking from fifteen years of age, during the dinner hour allowed at the Munition Works openly in the streets, walking to and from their work'.

Other local firms engaged on government contracts, Minty's and Barlow & Alden's, for example, also had female employees. Eleven women, including the aptly-named Miss Sparks, were working as electricians for Hill, Upton & Co by 1917, and *The Oxford Times* was 'trying a lady in the reporters' room' in April 1916 after twenty-one men had enlisted.

A wounded soldier crosses Carfax in style, October 1914. Private cars, buses and hansom cabs were initially used to ferry patients from the railway station to the Third Southern General Hospital, but the number of casualties soon made ambulances essential.

Chapter Four

News from the Front Line

DURING THE BATTLE OF THE SOMME in July 1916, 'Watcher' in the *Oxford Chronicle* noted that the casualty lists revealed 'the sacrifice of young men in all ranks and social classes'. An old college servant had lamented a few days earlier: 'All our best men are falling'. Whether serving in the county regiments or elsewhere, Oxonians were involved in a vast struggle which seemed unending and beyond comprehension. For most of them, the trenches of the Western Front formed the battleground, but many saw action in other theatres of war, or in the Royal Navy or the air force.

The conditions in which they lived, fought, and, in many cases

Good Luck and Safe Return, a poem by Henry Taunt in one of his wartime cards for men at the front. The card provided space for a loved one's photograph which Taunt would doubtless be happy to supply.

became casualties of war, were often appalling, but the shared misery inspired a remarkable camaraderie and made more precious those periods of rest and recreation behind the lines.

Both the Ox and Bucks and the Oxfordshire Hussars were soon heavily involved in the fighting. The 2nd Battalion Ox and Bucks disembarked at Boulogne on 14 August, and arrived in front of Mons in Belgium on the 23rd, just a day after the first shots of the war by British soldiers. The following day, Sir John French, Commander-in-Chief of the British Expeditionary Force, ordered a retreat towards the French frontier, and, despite a terrific rearguard action, Allied forces were forced south of the River Aisne by 30 August. By this time, however, the impetus of the German advance was waning and the 2nd Battalion took part in the successful Allied counter-attack beginning on 5 September which drove enemy forces back across the River Marne and the River Aisne.

The British Expeditionary Force had time to move to Flanders before Antwerp fell on 15 October and fought in the crucial First Battle of Ypres beginning on 19 October when the German army tried, and failed, to reach the French Channel coast.

Captain Henry Dillon, of the 2nd Battalion Ox and Bucks recalled a fierce attack at the Battle of Langemarck near Ypres on 23 October 1914:

> 'A great grey mass of humanity was charging straight on us not 50 yards off ... for one short minute or two we poured the ammunition into them in boxfuls. My rifles were red hot at the finish, I know, and that was the end of the battle for me. The firing died down and out of the darkness a great moan came.'

The 2nd Battalion fought its most celebrated action of the war in Nonne Bosschen Wood on 11 November when the Prussian Guard was routed.

The Oxfordshire Hussars were nearly sent to Egypt at the end of August 1914, and then went to a training camp at Churn. Following the intervention of Winston Churchill, First Lord of the Admiralty, they were sent at short notice to Dunkirk on 20 September as the cavalry support for a planned operation by marines at Antwerp. In early October only a few members of the regiment accompanied the marines and the remainder busied themselves with training and games of football. The officers hunted with beagles and went off joy-riding in private cars which they had brought with them; one party reached the front line on the Menin road, and swiftly retired! This enjoyable interlude ended abruptly on 31 October when dismounted men were ordered into the hard-fought Battle of Ypres. They helped to defend the Wytschaete-Messines ridge for nearly two days and thus prevented a German breakthrough. Sir John French later paid particular tribute to the gallantry of the Oxfordshire Hussars who were among the first Territorial troops to fight in the war.

The Germans' Schlieffen Plan had envisaged seizing Paris and forcing France to capitulate within six weeks. It had clearly failed, but German forces now occupied most of Belgium, and France had lost around ten per cent of its territory and a third of its industrial capacity. Military stalemate had been achieved and both sides began to dig in along a 460-mile front between the North Sea and the Swiss frontier. The Germans generally held the higher ground, enabling them to dig more deeply before reaching the water table. Their trench-lines were highly defensive in character, seeking to protect territorial gains which the Allies were eager to recapture. The war had become 'a form of siege in which for cavalry mounted action would be impossible'.

Allied commanders still envisaged the cavalry exploiting gaps in the German defences created by the artillery and the infantry, but the Oxfordshire Hussars waited in vain for such an opportunity during the Battle of Loos in 1915, the Battle of the Somme in 1916, and again at the Battle of Arras in 1917. When tanks did help to create an initial breakthrough at the Battle of Cambrai in December 1917, slow communications seem to have fatally delayed implementation of plans for three supporting cavalry divisions to sweep through the gap. Cavalry regiments continued to train, and to look after their horses as best they could, but for much of the time the men supported the infantry in the trenches or acted as navvies on construction projects such as the building of light railways.

Before the Oxfordshire Hussars first went into the trenches at Zillebeke in February 1915, their training for trench warfare included bomb-throwing – 'very crude and home-made articles generally constructed out of an empty jar or tin'. 'Bombs' or hand grenades were already proving more important than rifles in the trenches and the British were still developing them at this stage. The regiment was in

Men of the Oxfordshire Hussars in the trenches, June 1915. The cavalry waited in vain for opportunities to exploit breakthroughs in the trench warfare and dismounted soldiers had to serve in the lines and join working parties like the infantry.

the trenches at Vermelles for the first two months of 1916, and, in May 1917, after the Battle of Arras, it went into trenches at Guillemont Farm. German bombardments caused serious casualties at Guillemont – Major Valentine Fleming, MP for South Oxfordshire, was killed on 20 May – but the period was notable too for a successful raid on the German trenches, and the subsequent defence of that position.

Part of the regiment was at Cote Wood near Hargicourt in December, and the men celebrated Christmas Day with bully-beef and plum pudding in the trenches. The officers did rather better:

'We had a sumptuous Christmas dinner – soup, tinned herrings, a pheasant, some beef, an excellent ration plum-pudding lit up

Second Lieutenant H.A. Le Mesurier of the Ox and Bucks uses a trench periscope, 1915. Excellent German sniper fire meant that it could be fatal to raise your head above the parapet.

with burning rum, and sherry, burgundy, and brandy to drink
... It was an awful night out, and a lot of snow fell, but inside
our hut we were as warm as toast.'

The Oxfordshire Hussars continued to be split into different parties in
early 1918, and twenty men from one such group were killed in the
battle for Rifle Wood near Domart-sur-la-Luce on 1 April which helped
to check the great German offensive. As the Allies successfully counter-
attacked in August 1918, the cavalry was suddenly needed again and
the Oxfordshire Hussars supported the infantry of 6 Brigade in the final
months of the war. Mounted patrols from the regiment were the first
British troops to enter the Belgian towns of Mauberge on 9 November
and Erquelinnes two days later on Armistice Day.

Most of the fighting strength of the Ox and Bucks served on the
Western Front for the duration of the war. The 2nd Battalion fought at
the Battle of Festubert in May 1915, and took part in an attack at
Givenchy in September during the Battle of Loos. The regiment was
involved in some of the subsidiary battles on the Somme in 1916, and
played a significant role in the Battle of Arras in late April 1917. In the
later stages of the Battle of Cambrai in December, when the Germans
launched a strong counter-attack, the battalion's action at Lock 6 on
the Canal du Nord enabled a successful British withdrawal. In August
1918, the regiment captured Sapignies, near Bapaume, as the Allies
gained the initiative, and in the autumn it took part in the battles which
saw the Germans pushed back beyond the Hindenburg Line.

The 1/4th, or 1st Territorial, Battalion landed at Boulogne on 30
March 1915, and had its first experience of railway trucks marked
'Hommes (Men) 40 Chevaux (Horses) 8' on the way to the front. By
the end of April, the men were in the trenches in front of Ploegsteert
Wood, known to British Tommies as 'Plug Street Wood,' and they were
soon issued with primitive gas masks, cotton waste pads and goggles,
following the Germans' first use of gas at Ypres. The battalion was in
the trenches at Festubert from May 1915 until August 1916, and fought
in an action at Albert in late July 1916 during the Battle of the Somme.
In April 1917, the battalion suffered heavy losses in an attack on
Guillemont Farm, and in August it lost 97 men killed and 163 wounded
during the Third Battle of Ypres (or Passchendaele).

In November 1917 the 1/4th was ordered to Italy to help counter an anticipated Austrian attack. The 2/4th Battalion reached France on 24 May 1916, and took part in its first raid in late June, incurring numerous casualties. It was mainly involved in trench warfare – a stray shell killed Lieutenant Reginald Tiddy in August – and in supporting actions such as the raid at Fayet, near St Quentin on 28 April 1917 when Sergeant Major Brooks earned the regiment's first VC of the war.

Company Sergeant Major Edward Brooks VC in 1917. A Headington resident, Brooks served in the 2/4th Battalion Ox and Bucks and was awarded the Victoria Cross for conspicuous bravery during a raid at Foyet on 28 April 1917.

HERO'S WELCOME

During the summer of 1917 news that the Victoria Cross had been awarded to Company Sergeant Major Edward Brooks created huge excitement in Oxford and Headington, and in Oakley, Buckinghamshire, his birthplace.

Brooks received the award from King George V at a ceremony in Buckingham Palace on Saturday, 21 July 1917, and returned to a hero's welcome in Oxford. The Mayor, Alderman Sir Robert Buckell, and Corporation met him off the train at Oxford station. In a welcoming speech, the Mayor remarked:

> 'You have won honours for your native place and for Oxford, and we are proud of this honour which we in a measure share with your deeds and valour.'

Brooks was conducted outside where a horse-drawn coach provided by Mrs G.H. Morrell of Headington Hill Hall was waiting. The coach, preceded by Headington Silver Band, drove through cheering crowds in central Oxford, where patriotic flags flew from shops and public buildings. The press of people was perhaps even greater as Brooks reached Headington, and a policeman asked children to stay behind the rope. One boy was heard to remark: 'Wait till I'm a sergeant major, the police won't think they are so mighty then.'

Colonel Hoole made the grounds of Headington Manor available for a well-attended reception. The Mayor spoke again, and, after the band had played the *Marseillaise*, Brooks was presented with an illuminated address and over £108 raised by friends and neighbours. To conclude the proceedings, the Headington Silver Band played 'When the Boys Come Home' and the National Anthem.

Mrs Fry, who had lost her husband in the raid where Brooks won the Victoria Cross, attended the reception, and 'her mourning-clad figure and that of the hero of the afternoon with his purple ribbon ... made a little microcosm of the glory and the tragedy of war.'

The 2/4th fought in the later stages of the Battle of Arras, and then took part in the Third Battle of Ypres in August and September 1917, losing many men. Back in the trenches by October, the 2/4th was overwhelmed during the German offensive in March 1918. Merged with the similarly depleted Bucks Battalion and with fresh troops from England, the battalion helped to fight off another German attack at the Battle of the Lys in April. The 2/4th earned a second VC on 12 September when Lance Corporal Alfred Wilcox put four machine guns out of action during the battalion's attack on Junction Post.

The 7th and 8th Service Battalions of the Ox and Bucks, raised at Cowley Barracks, landed in France in September 1915. In just seven weeks, the 7th lost eleven men killed and thirty-two wounded, before both battalions were transferred to Salonika in November.

The diversion of British and French troops to Salonika in neutral Greece was in support of Serbia which was invaded by Austria-Hungary on 5 October 1915. Bulgaria joined the attack on Serbia on the 9th in a bid to seize Macedonia, and an initial French advance northwards from Salonika

Officers of the 7th (Service) Battalion Ox and Bucks in Salonika, 1917. The 7th and 8th Battalions were sent from France to Salonika in November 1915 and spent the rest of the war in what was popularly thought to be a sideshow.

was soon checked. The 7th and 8th Battalions arrived to find the Allied forces in a difficult situation, struggling to create defences around Salonika, the so-called 'Birdcage Line,' in appalling weather, and in the face of 'the sub-hostile attitude of the inhabitants'. The 8th Battalion was a designated Pioneer battalion, primarily intended for construction work of all kinds, but both battalions were heavily occupied digging trenches and road-making.

In August 1916 men from the 7th Battalion were the first British troops to fight their way on to Serbian soil at Horseshoe Hill, but Bulgarian forces repelled an attack on the Petit Couronné in April 1917, inflicting heavy casualties. There was virtual stalemate after this, and the Germans described Salonika as 'their greatest prisoner-of-war camp' because so many Allied troops were pinned down there; in Britain, there was talk of the 'Salonika Picnic Party.' At last, on 15 September, 1918, the Allied army, reinforced now by Serb and Greek forces, began a decisive assault which led to the capitulation of Bulgaria on the 30th. Men from the 7th Battalion, though weakened

Officers' mess of the 1st Battalion Ox and Bucks at Ezra's Tomb beside the River Tigris, 1915. The battalion was part of an ill-fated expedition against Turkish forces by the 6th Indian Division which ended in humiliating surrender at Kut in April 1916.

by malaria and short rations, claimed to be the first Britons to enter Bulgaria on 25 September.

Battalions of the Ox and Bucks also fought in Mesopotamia and Italy. British interests in the Persian Gulf and Mesopotamia had been paramount for decades, but German influence in Turkey had led to approval for a Berlin to Baghdad railway, scotching the dream of a Baghdad to India line and threatening British prestige and oilfields. Once Turkey joined the war in November 1914, an expeditionary force, including the 1st Battalion Ox and Bucks, the old 43rd Regiment, was sent from India to protect British interests in Mesopotamia.

The Turkish forces proved stronger than expected, and the climate was hostile, but the expeditionary force fought its way to within thirty miles of Baghdad, and secured a victory at Ctesiphon on 22 November 1915. With insufficient men to tackle Turkish reinforcements, General Townshend retreated to Kut-al-Amara, where a long siege began on 7

December. A relieving force suffered heavy losses trying to reach Kut, and T.E. Lawrence and Aubrey Herbert were unable to negotiate the ransom and release of the garrison before it surrendered on 29 April 1916. The 13,000 survivors, including some 287 officers and men of the 1st Battalion, were marched off into captivity. Many men died on the way to work camps on the Berlin to Baghdad railway and contact with the surviving prisoners was not established until February 1917. In the meantime, a re-formed 1st Battalion was part of the relieving force which captured Baghdad in March 1917 and seized Hit on the Euphrates in February 1918, remaining there until the end of the war.

Italy joined the Allies as the Gallipoli landings began in April 1915, anticipating territorial gains at the expense of both Austria-Hungary and Turkey. The Italians achieved some initial success but they were

Officers of the 1/4th Battalion Ox and Bucks in Italy, 1918. After serving in France, the battalion was transferred to Italy in November 1917 in anticipation of a major Austrian attack which finally took place on 15 June 1918.

forced back some sixty miles to the line of the River Piave by November 1917. Eight Anglo-French divisions, including the 1/4th Battalion and the 1/1st Bucks Battalion Ox and Bucks, were quickly transferred from the Western Front to provide reinforcements. The long-anticipated Austrian attack, by 106 divisions, came on 15 June 1918 and it was soon beaten back, albeit with heavy losses. The 1/4th lost six officers and forty-two men, and two officers and ninety-two men were wounded; Captain Edward Brittain, Vera Brittain's brother, was one of the officers killed. The Allies launched an offensive against the Austrians in October, giving the 1/4th opportunities to raid enemy positions, and finally, on 3 November, to accept the surrender of a battalion and a half.

The four Oxfordshire Heavy Batteries were serving with the Royal Garrison Artillery on the Western Front by June 1916. A diary compiled in the 1920s by A.R. Wilkins, formerly a corporal in the 128th (Oxfordshire) Heavy Battery, Royal Garrison Artillery, describes the work of that unit which landed at Le Havre in March 1916.

It was sent straight to the Ypres Salient and took over the old guns and equipment of the 108th Battery. When called upon to fire for twenty-nine hours at the end of April, men had to pour water down the muzzles of some guns because they were over-heating. The battery was behind the lines but always at risk from bombardment if spotted by enemy planes. At the Battle of Messines in June 1917 the battery fired 5,515 rounds, beginning a bombardment at 3.10am when Hill 60 was to be blown up. The artillery employed the creeping barrage technique and some soldiers strayed too far ahead falling victim to friendly fire. The 128th provided artillery support at the Third Battle of Ypres between August and November, firing well over 3,000 shells, some thirty-seven per cent of them gas shells. The unit left the Ypres Salient in November, but only to face the great German offensive in March 1918 when it was forced into confused retreat. From 8 August, the 128th supported the Allied assault, but Wilkins was wounded and 'sorry to miss the end'.

Many Oxonians and University men enlisted in, or were allocated to, other regiments or joined the Navy or the Royal Flying Corps. Frank Turner, from Blackfriars Road, became a stoker in the Royal Navy, and was the only man from his mess to survive when HMS *Aboukir* was

Men from one of the Oxfordshire Heavy Batteries serving with the Royal Garrison Artillery in France, July 1917. Four City Police officers are among the group, Sergeants Webb and Brockland, and Constables Webb and Edmunds.

torpedoed in the North Sea in September 1914.

Ronald Poulton-Palmer, the son of Professor Poulton and a brilliant Varsity athlete who played rugby for England, was commissioned into the Royal Berkshire Regiment as lieutenant and was killed by a sniper's bullet at Ploegsteert Wood in April 1915, the first officer in his battalion to die. Another professor's son, Alasdair McDonnell, joined the Ox and Bucks at the outset, but he was commissioned as second lieutenant in the Cameron Highlanders, his ambition being to 'let a Hun meet a Highlander in a true hand-to-hand fight'; sadly, he was killed in March 1915. Lieutenant E.H. Pember, the son of Francis Pember, Warden of All Souls College, was commissioned in the Royal Field Artillery in

Portrait of Captain Noel Chavasse VC. Oxford-born Chavasse was attached to the Liverpool Scottish Regiment as a doctor. He was the only man during the war to receive two Victoria Crosses, for exceptional bravery in treating wounded soldiers, the second one awarded after his death at the Third Battle of Ypres in August 1917.
Taylor Library

1915, volunteered for the RFC in the autumn of 1916, and was killed while taking reconnaissance photographs in September 1917. Captain John Liddell, another RFC pilot, was awarded the Victoria Cross in July 1915 after flying his aircraft back from a reconnaissance mission despite injuries which led to his death.

Noel Chavasse, who was born in Oxford and educated at Magdalen College School and Trinity College, joined the Royal Army Medical Corps before the war and was attached to the 10th Battalion the King's Liverpool Regiment, the Liverpool Scottish. He received a VC at Guillemont in August 1916 for repeatedly going into no man's land under fire to rescue the wounded. A witness, Frederick Jackson, recalled:

'That night, Dr Chavasse went out into no man's land with his devoted stretcher-bearers, looking for wounded men and bringing them in. The amazing thing about this rescue exploit was that he carried and used his electric torch as he walked about between the trenches, whistling and calling out to wounded men to indicate their whereabouts, and so be brought in. Ignoring the snipers' bullets and any sporadic fusillade, he carried on with his work of succour throughout the hours of darkness.'

At the Third Battle of Ypres in 1917, Chavasse was injured and ultimately killed at his post, again trying to save as many lives as possible. He was posthumously awarded a second VC, the only man to win the medal twice during the Great War. (Appendix Table 3 lists

T.E. Lawrence in Arab dress, a portrait by Henry Chase, 1918. Brought up and educated in Oxford, Lawrence was sent to Cairo as an intelligence officer because of his knowledge of the Arab world. His exploits leading the Arab revolt against the Turks made him the romantic war hero, Lawrence of Arabia.

all the Oxford VCs).

Admiral Sir Reginald Tyrwhitt, born in Oxford in 1870 and a naval cadet at the age of 13, was also viewed as a local hero, who led his Harwich

LAWRENCE OF ARABIA

Thomas Edward Lawrence (1888-1935) was born at Tremadoc in Wales, the second of five sons of Thomas Chapman and Sarah Junner. The couple moved to Oxford in 1896 and lived as Mr and Mrs Lawrence at 2 Polstead Road. Ned attended the City of Oxford High School for Boys between 1896 and 1907 and gained a First in History at Jesus College, Oxford in 1910.

A keen archaeologist, Lawrence worked on excavations at Carchemish in Syria between 1911 and early 1914, learning Arabic and becoming immersed in the Arab world. After Turkey joined the war, Lawrence was posted to Cairo as an intelligence officer in December 1914 and served in the 'Arab Bureau'. In April 1916, he undertook an abortive mission to negotiate the release of the besieged Anglo-Indian army at Kut.

Lawrence helped to plan the Arab uprising against the Turks which began in June 1916, and he assessed the military situation at Jiddah in October. He convinced Arab leaders, including Emir Feisal and his superiors that Arab forces were best suited to guerrilla warfare. Lawrence became Feisal's liaison officer and adopted Arab dress for practical as well as ideological reasons. He and his Arab followers seized the port of Aqaba in June 1917 and harassed Turkish forces by attacking the railway line between Medina and Damascus.

In September 1918 Lawrence's forces defeated the Turks at Deraa, and he hoped to reach Damascus before General Allenby's regular army. His arrival, in a Rolls-Royce and accompanied by Indian lancers, came hours after Australian cavalry had entered the city.

Exhausted by campaigning in extreme conditions, Lawrence felt that the Arabs were being betrayed by Allied plans to partition the Ottoman Empire. Allenby sent him home on leave, a full colonel and a hero whose exploits soon became the stuff of legend.

Oxford men in the Royal Navy, May 1916. Standing, left to right: W.J. Wells, J. Whittaker, A.H. Coleman; sitting, F. Shrimpton, A.H. Boyes, R.G. Alder.

force in many wartime actions and received the surrender of German U-boats after the Armistice.

Oxford men served in virtually every theatre of the war. William Mitchell, who had worked for the High Street jeweller's, Walford & Spokes, became Chief Petty Officer in the Armoured Car Squadron, serving in Romania and elsewhere on the Eastern Front before being killed while supporting Russian forces in Galicia in July 1917. Lieutenant Duncan Elliott was with an 800-strong force in northern Nigeria in November 1914, and Sergeant Wilfrid Sanders, from Holywell Street, served with British forces in German East Africa from 1916, meeting up with other Oxonians in the Machine Gun Corps. He reported in May 1917 that 'tho' the Hun is beleaguered and short of supplies, he has still plenty of fight left'.

In April 1917, men in the Royal Army Medical Corps who had been at the Third Southern General Hospital in Oxford, wrote of their experiences in Egypt, and invited others to 'come out and see the world for nothing'. Private Ray Wilson, who had emigrated from Oxford to

Australia, was in the firing line at Gallipoli with the Australian Light Horse in August 1915. Another Oxford emigrant, Private Gerald Duck, whose mother lived in Warneford Road, was also with the Australians at Gallipoli. A Bible in his pocket saved him from serious injury there in September 1915 but he was killed in France in August 1918. Private Christopher Choldcroft, the son of a Woodstock Road hairdresser, had emigrated to Canada for his health in 1913, but he joined the Canadian forces and was killed by shellfire in France in 1916.

Most men experienced the war through the trenches on the Western Front, which were little more than a hundred miles from Oxford at their nearest point. There was nothing new about trench warfare, but the scale and duration of this struggle was quite novel. The trenches dug in the early stages of the war were steadily improved with better parapets, duckboards and timberwork to prevent collapses. Behind the front line ran a parallel support line, and, by 1915, there was usually a parallel reserve line further back. These lines were connected at intervals by short communication trenches.

Dug-outs made life for front line troops slightly safer and less uncomfortable, and, as artillery power increased, concrete block-houses began to be used. The British trenches were 'wet, cold, smelly, and generally squalid', designed with a view to an early break-out. Private C. Summerfield of the 2nd Battalion Ox and Bucks reported in November 1914:

> 'We are living in the ground like rabbits, and having our food the best we can. We might be having a snap (sic) when a shell comes over and cuts the dirt all over our food: then we say something I can tell you.'

Captain E.S. Kemp, from Magdalen College, described trench life in the Ypres salient:

> 'We lived in ditches literally over our knees in water all the time ... I remember we drank for some days the water out of a shell hole and found at the end a corpse at the bottom of it.'

In August 1915, Private Alec Wiblin complained that men had to take turns out in the pouring rain because of the lack of space in their dug-out. A member of the 1/4th Battalion Ox and Bucks described the water in the trenches as being so deep that 'some fellows found the most comfortable way of going about to be with only shirt and boots on'. At night, an Oxford Territorial was disturbed when a great rat knocked three tins from a shelf above his head and he regularly had mice running over his face and chest. Lice were a perpetual problem, and men spent spare moments trying to kill them. Occasionally, soldiers would be marched off to a bath-house in a converted brewery where they wallowed in huge vats of hot water and exchanged dirty clothes for clean ones.

In the circumstances, complaining became something of an art form, and Second Lieutenant Frederick Whitlock of the 6th Battalion Ox and Bucks said of his men:

> 'They grouse when food is not as plentiful as they have known it, they grouse at being made to work all night and half the day, but their hearts are in the right place, and they'll do honour to the old country yet.'

Major Rose marvelled that 'the British "Tommy", who, exhausted and "fed-up" at night, was heard singing and wood chopping the next morning, as if wherever he was were the best place in the world.' The Carfax Copper, on duty in all weathers, became an unlikely source of humour for Oxford men in rain-soaked trenches who would greet each other by saying, 'think of the poor policeman at Carfax'. Sergeant Hydra Sorrell of the Wiltshire Regiment even came up with a poem about him:

'If we're stuck in the trenches for hours without rest,
And are jawed by the sergeant, a grumpy old pest,
Or do endless fatigues, we've found that it's best
To think of the policeman at Carfax.'

The trench lines offered some protection from snipers' bullets and bombardments but trench warfare involved not only battles and raids against enemy positions but also regular fatigue, or working, parties which put the soldier's life at more deadly risk. Second Lieutenant Whitlock described one such duty on a night in September 1915 when he supervised fifty men digging trenches in the open just 150 yards from a German position with bullets whistling overhead.

As the war progressed, long range artillery and bombing by enemy aircraft posed an increasing threat to men well behind the lines. In May

1918, for example, Lieutenant William Fleet, Magdalen College's first American Rhodes Scholar, was among those killed when their billets were bombed after they had spent an evening celebrating the end of a tour of duty. Around 7,000 British officers and men were killed or wounded daily during the war even when the front was comparatively quiet. Writing to the President of Magdalen, his old college, Captain E.S. Kemp of the 23rd Royal Fusiliers reported that by February 1916 'nearly every original fighting man of my platoon had gone and this though we had never been in any attack or had to stand one'.

The 5th Battalion Ox and Bucks suffered 433 casualties, including 63 killed, within three months of landing in France in May 1915; the 6th Battalion had nearly 300 casualties despite being in no important engagement. Death became almost commonplace but men were still badly affected when a friend or popular officer was killed. The parents of Lieutenant Reginald Herbert, an Oxford man in the London Regiment, were told that his men wept when they learned of his death on 21 May 1917. A soldier serving with the 1/4th Ox and Bucks expressed his regrets in March 1916 for a 'decent old boy I liked very much blown to atoms in his billet a few hours ago...'

Communication between the trenches and home was surprisingly quick and easy – letters and parcels took between two and four days. Field Postcards providing the most basic details were one way of keeping in touch, and Captain Roger Dixey, serving with the Royal Field Artillery, sent his mother, Isabel, in Oxford as many as forty-six from France between July and December 1915. In return, she sent him comforts as recorded in her diary on 23 September 1915:

> 'Got sulphur soap, tobacco, notebook, choc[olate], soup, brand's lozenges, ginger to make 3lb parcel for R, which F. posted at G.P.O.'

Men's letters were censored to ensure that no secrets were given away, and the Censor even deleted a passage in Greek from a letter sent from the front by a former Mansfield College student in May 1915. Correspondents generally tried to be reassuring, and Jack Buckland, from Church Street, St Ebbe's, serving with the Ox and Bucks, wrote to his parents in September 1914:

> 'I am enjoying myself a treat out here. It was just what I was wishing for, something nice and exciting ... I don't suppose we

shall be out here very long as the Germans are losing hundreds every day, so you need not worry.'

In February 1917, Sergeant H. Godfrey wrote home to his mother at 59 Lime Walk, Headington:

'Just a line to let you know I am still quite well and am using the advantage of a green envelope to let you have a little news. Please let Aunt Harriett know I received her parcel quite safely and the cake and cocoa was a treat (it always is in the line) as rations are not so plentiful and we know what it is to crave for water even in this cold weather ... tomorrow 16.2.17 we are off up the line for another large "Stunt" on a very large scale, one whole Division going over the top in an attack. My Company is in the front wave, so don't be surprised the next time I write I am on my way to "Blighty".'

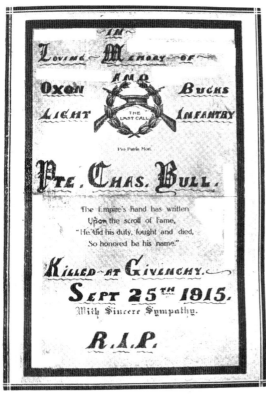

His hopes for a cushy 'Blighty' wound that would have seen him back in England were sadly unrealised and he was killed just two days later at the age of 21.

A few of the individuals and families devastated by news of the loss of loved ones later established that they were prisoners of war. In July 1915, the father of Freddy Fitzwygram wrote to Herbert Warren, the President of Magdalen College: 'I cannot express how thankful we feel he has been spared.' Freddy, for his part, wrote to Warren from prison hospital in Dusseldorf: 'We get all the official communiqués here, so we have a fair idea of the general situation, but it is

Memorial card decorated and sent home to Oxford by Private Charles Bull's brother, 1915.

rather strange seeing the war through German spectacles; the contrast is certainly remarkable.'

A total of 1,228 men from Oxfordshire and Buckinghamshire military units became prisoners of war, 856 in Germany, 319 in Turkey, 42 in Austria and 11 in Bulgaria. The highest number of prisoners, 756, was taken in 1918 during the great German offensive. Some 276 of these men died in captivity, most of them in Turkey, where other prisoners only survived in 1916-7 through the good offices of the United States Consul and American citizens.

Through the Red Cross, an effective support system was established for prisoners of war, and regular food and clothing parcels were sent out. A bakery in Switzerland supplied bread to prisoners in Germany on a regular basis. Prisoners seem generally to have been well treated, and a private in the Oxfordshire and Buckinghamshire Light Infantry who had been injured at Givenchy in September 1915 praised the kindness of staff in his prison hospital. Nursing sisters had brought them treats and sung carols on Christmas Day:

> 'The singing was beautiful, for they have lovely voices. It regularly thrills you to hear them sing. Nobody would ever believe we were fighting them, for they are so good in their ways.'

Local men in a German prisoner of war camp at Burgsteinfurt in Westphalia, November 1918.

At Ankara in Turkey in 1917-8, Godfrey Elton, a Balliol man with the 4th Hampshire Regiment, admired the nearby ruins, but felt no responsibility for them because 'we have a professional archaeologist with us (Woolley, ex New College)'. Instead, he spent his time 'reading masses of modern history, all I can get, and have written a little poetry, and a lot of prose'. Inevitably, there was criticism of prison rations, and Private Ashmall, from Randolph Street, described the German food in 1917 as 'positively awful' – black bread, chestnut soup and crushed maize plus black coffee three times a day. Some prisoners in Germany were set to work on farms, at baker's shops or butcher's. There were some escape attempts, and, in March 1917, Captain Godsal of the Ox and Bucks and another officer reached the Dutch frontier after jumping from a train while their guard was asleep. A Corpus Christi man, George Seel, recounted how he and another nine officers escaped by tunnel from their prison camp in Breslau,and headed for Switzerland in pairs. All were captured in Austria and imprisoned in a camp near Vienna. Their money was sent on from Germany and each of their pass-books bore the note:

> 'May 21. To repay of kitchen-damages the out-breaking of English officer-prisoners-of-war, 18 marks 35 pfennigs.'

Chapter 5

While You're Away

OXFORD WAS ENERGISED from the very beginning of the war. Women, and those men who remained, organised fund-raising committees and voluntary work parties, and took the lead in clubs which entertained troops and wounded soldiers. Older men and boys prepared to defend the city against enemy attacks. German sympathies ebbed away, but cosmopolitan Oxford continued to have an international outlook, focused especially on the refugees and suffering populations of Allied countries. The threat of air raids led swiftly to measures which darkened Oxford's streets and shops for four years. Later in the war, food rationing, cultivating allotments, saving fuel and recycling provided extra challenges. Oxford inevitably became a less frivolous place and wartime restrictions curbed excessive drinking, but a dislocated society offered new temptations.

Women of position, as *The Times* noted, played a huge role in the war effort and there were many such women – academics, dons' wives, undergraduates, and ladies of independent means – in Oxford and particularly in North Oxford. They soon became involved in a plethora of good causes, making comforts for the troops, providing military hospitals with essential supplies, organising relief for Allied prisoners of war, running clubs and canteens for soldiers, and fund-raising on a grand scale. Queen Mary issued an appeal for women to take up their needles on 4 August 1914 and Mrs Gamlen held a meeting at her house in Banbury Road on the 13th to form an Oxford branch of Queen Mary's Needlework Guild. The 112 members of the branch eventually contributed 39,514 garments, but the Guild also raised funds to buy materials for other workers. Brasenose College made 22 High Street available as a central depot for the receipt of finished clothes that were then sent on to the headquarters in St James's Palace. The Oxford Branch helped to co-ordinate the work of other working parties that grew up in the city. By the middle of August, for example, women of 'all classes', and even, it was said, several German girls, were making

Women volunteers make bandages and dressings for the Third Southern General Hospital at the Institute of Forestry in Parks Road, February 1917. In other rooms, women were busy mending clothes and linen and making splints and slings for the hospital.

clothes for soldiers in a temporary workroom at the University Museum.

A city working party met on three afternoons a week at the Police Court in the Town Hall. Ladies subscribed money for materials and did sewing and cutting out as well as teaching poor women and putting right any defects in their work. Women at a University Press working party made mufflers for members of the Press who had joined the Army. Another group of ladies, supervised by Lady Osler and Miss Courtenay-Bell, occupied the School of Forestry in Parks Road, supplying dressings, bandages, slings and papier maché splints to the military hospitals, as well as mending clothes and hospital linen.

Work of this kind could also be done in the home – Isabel Dixey spent 8 July 1915 quietly at home working at respirator pockets, and trainee teachers at Cherwell Hall whiled away their evenings knitting mittens, body-belts and socks. In May 1915, Constance and Eleanor Butler appealed for funds to send food and tobacco to Oxford prisoners of war who were not covered by the Ox and Bucks regimental scheme because they had enlisted in other regiments. They established an office at 4a Magdalen Street, courtesy of the music seller, Mr Taphouse, and sent out more than 100 parcels by October. When these two schemes were merged at the end of 1916, the Butlers and other women involved transferred their attention to the Oxford Comforts Fund for Wounded Soldiers and joined the Archdeacon of Oxford in a new appeal. The money raised was used to supplement the diets of patients at the Third Southern General Hospital and arrange outings for them. A fruit and flower depot opened at 55a High Street on the same day as the hospital, receiving gifts to brighten the wards and provide the men with fruit. Appealing for further support in February 1915, Doris Thomson reported that gifts of fruit had come from as far afield as South Africa, Canada and the West Indies. Patients initially lacked more basic foods, and, until the Government decided to supply better breakfasts to patients in January 1917, the Third Southern General Hospital had an Egg Secretary who issued regular appeals. The children of Cowley St John Girls' School sent a weekly supply of eggs, and thirty-seven wounded soldiers wrote thanking them in February 1916.

Women students from St Hilda's College sang at Sunday evening services at the hospital and wheeled convalescing patients out in bath chairs or took them on river trips. In October 1916 Frances Spooner, wife of the Warden of New College, and a team of ladies began a scheme through which bed-bound wounded soldiers undertook therapeutic embroidery work. Regimental crests proved to be the most popular subject, but men also produced belts, mats and rugs, and in June 1917 one of the prize-winning entries at an exhibition in Mansfield College was a view of Worcester College from the garden.

Other women were keen to undertake hands-on nursing; May Cannan, daughter of the Secretary of the University Press and a wartime employee there, became a Voluntary Aid Detachment nurse in her spare time. On 6 August 1914 H.W.B. Joseph found Mrs Haldane, the wife of the scientist, J.S. Haldane, busy organising a class of women who wished to be trained for Red Cross work.

Canteens and clubs to cater for soldiers and their relatives and for hospital patients proliferated in wartime Oxford and most depended mainly on women. As Oxford filled with recruits in September 1914, the Mayor called on Mrs Grundy, the wife of G.B. Grundy, Fellow of Corpus Christi College, and 'asked her whether she and some friends of hers could provide a supper every day at the town hall for some hundreds of men, the first of which should take place within twenty-four hours'. They achieved this tall order, and Mrs Grundy later helped with the catering at the Third Southern General Hospital before organising food control in the city.

Emily Poulton, wife of Professor E.B. Poulton, was behind the Union Jack Club in Church Street, St Ebbe's which opened in November 1914 as a meeting place for the mothers and wives of serving soldiers. By November 1916 the club had over eighty members who could talk, knit or sew, and enjoy teas and suppers at a low cost while their children played upstairs in a staffed nursery. Helen Wicks, of 115 Banbury Road, organised the Garden Club for Wounded Soldiers at Mansfield College which opened in May 1916. It was originally intended as a summer-time open air venture, but the college provided rooms during the winter and the club supplied 105,000 free teas within eighteen months. A Catholic Soldiers' Club opened at 12 Turl Street in December 1915 and there was another social club for soldiers at 43a Queen Street, but the Young Men's Christian Association (YMCA) was the main wartime provider of recreation facilities for soldiers and cadets.

Men in uniform automatically held war membership of the YMCA and the main building at 10 George Street provided a lounge, library, billiard room, plunge and shower baths, entertainments, debates and religious services for which attendance was voluntary. By December 1914 the YMCA was providing a buffet at Cowley Barracks and a 'little

Wounded soldiers, with women helpers, enjoy a concert at the Young Men's Christian Association premises in George Street, April 1915. The YMCA played a vital recreational role in wartime Oxford, with huts at Cowley Barracks and the Ashhurst War Hospital as well as central club rooms.

tin hut in the field' opposite the barracks was opened in 1915. A voluntary committee of ladies led by Mrs W. Betts supplied refreshments to thousands of visitors from October 1915 until the end of the war. The main building became so busy – soldiers were putting over 2,000 letters a week in the post box – that additional premises were acquired above 2 George Street in March 1916. Disaster struck in January 1917 when the main building was severely damaged by fire but temporary premises at 59-61 Cornmarket Street were secured and put into use within three days. Some rooms at 10 George Street were subsequently made usable and the YMCA opened additional buffets at the new recruiting office at 72 St Giles' and at the Ashhurst War Hospital in 1918. The organisation continued to be outward-looking, and Mrs Eva Whitmarsh, of 137 Woodstock Road, led an appeal for books and games for YMCA huts at the front in August 1917.

The Young Women's Christian Association (YWCA) opened an Oxford branch at 3 Magdalen Street in November 1916, providing a club room and hostel for women war workers. A canteen was added in May 1917, but demand soon exceeded capacity and Margaret Gardner announced the opening of larger premises at 72 St Giles' in April 1918.

Winning the war required money as well as manpower and women did much to raise funds for the war effort and encourage vital savings campaigns. Belgian Day on 7 November 1914 was Oxford's first major Flag Day. Mrs H.S. Kingerlee came up with the idea and Russell Brain, who had helped with similar events elsewhere, organised the event. Five hundred women made 90,000 bows before the day and many bows were sold from door to door; on the day itself, it was difficult to avoid the '600 fair sellers' of flags and badges on every street corner. A donkey and a decorated steam lorry provided rides, and a barrel organ played. In the evening, there was an open-air film show in Broad Street, the walls of Balliol College serving as the screen.

This event formed the prototype for a series of Flag Days, supporting for example, Britain's Allies, France, Russia and Italy, and the Red Cross. H.W.B. Joseph disapproved of 'being asked to buy a favour; it's not a mode of collecting I like' on Belgian Day, but this became standard practice. Indeed, an irate correspondent complained in the *Oxford Magazine* in June 1915:

'It is absurd, though it may be true, that some people will not subscribe for comforts for our wounded soldiers unless some young woman, clad in scanty white, flaunts into their faces her brazen charms.'

On Red Cross Day in June 1917, the *Oxford Chronicle* reported that 'the multitude of pretty girls in light summer frock[s] and shady hats lent quite a festive air to the proceedings'. The cosmopolitan nature of Oxford was indicated by a Russian Jews' Relief Fund Flag Day in July 1916 which raised around £350. In December 1915, Ellen Pope, of 60 Banbury Road, appealed on behalf of Italian troops fighting in the Alps, and Louise Vinogradoff, wife of Professor Paul Vinogradoff – who had left Moscow for England in 1901 – was collecting funds for Russian prisoners of war in November 1915.

Oxford formed a War Savings Committee in association with the National War Savings campaign in October 1916, and a central office was established at 15 Broad Street. By February 1917 there were forty-

Boy Scouts march past All Souls College with the Union Jack flying, June 1915. They were among the collectors for a Red Cross Day which included a military parade and an auction at the Martyrs' Memorial, and raised at least £1,875.

six War Savings Associations across the city formed in parishes, schools, colleges, clubs and workplaces. The Somerville College War Savings Association in 1917 had over ninety members who had bought 133 savings certificates. These associations, seventy-eight in number by March 1918, encouraged several thousand people to contribute to the National War Bonds Week, or Businessmen's Week, from 4-9 March when the city had the target of raising £150,000 for an 'Oxford' destroyer. A quarter scale model of a German pill-box was erected in St Giles', and a vast crowd gathered to watch a civic procession in which Boy Scouts played a prominent part. Cambridge had issued a friendly challenge to Oxford for the week, and a ladder installed at Carfax announced the sums received each day. In the event, Oxford outdid Cambridge by £361,512 to £276,386, helped by £15,000 from Messrs. Morris at Cowley. The savings campaign continued throughout 1918, and Feed the Guns Week in October raised almost £400,000, well above the target of £250,000.

As young men flocked to enlist in the first few days of the war, other men and boys were equally keen to play their part. Boy Scouts everywhere were quick to offer their services, and in Oxford they mobilised with a view to guarding and patrolling key sites such as

St Giles' Girls' School Empire Day parade in the playground, May 1916. Patriotic events took on a new significance in wartime, when school children's daily routine might include fund-raising activities, entertaining wounded soldiers and collecting horse chestnuts.

England's Day collectors outside a tobacconist's shop, April 1916. St George's flags and banners showing the mounted saint trampling the dragon encouraged patriotic giving and the day raised £600 for local war charities.

Feed the Guns Week procession in High Street, October 1918. The Bullnose Morris displayed a mine because Morris's Trench Warfare Factory in Cowley was turning out thousands of mine sinkers.

bridges and telegraph lines. Other proposed tasks included helping the families of servicemen, carrying messages, setting up first-aid posts and 'forwarding despatches dropped by aircraft'. Exeter College became their central office and during these early weeks they helped to set up the Third Southern General Hospital and guarded the guns of the University's Officer Training Corps at night.

Older men, including city councillors, enrolled as special constables at the police court during August 1914 and 166 of them were supplementing the depleted police force by March 1916. They had no uniform, but were issued with a whistle and a truncheon, and later, with an armlet. They patrolled in pairs, usually near their homes, and their main role was to assist the regular police, particularly during air raid alerts or civil disturbances.

The Oxford Volunteer Corps held its first drill in the University Parks on 13 August 1914 under the command of A.D. Godley, Fellow of Magdalen College and Public Orator, who was a former member of the University Volunteers. University men were prominent initially and they included Robert Bridges, the Poet Laureate, and seven professors. Sir Walter Raleigh, Professor of English Literature, would go straight from parades to meetings of the Delegates of the University Press, arriving 'cold, dirty, dishevelled but happy'. The Volunteer Corps started with twelve to fourteen members, but townsmen soon swelled the number to seventy or eighty and further platoons were established at Oxford University Press and in Headington. Like other such units established in the chaotic early weeks of the war, it was left to its own devices at first and men were simply issued with a brassard, a red armlet bearing the black letters GR for Georgius Rex. Inevitably, given their age, members were sometimes known as 'Gorgeous Wrecks', or 'Granny's Reserves'. The Oxford Volunteer Corps was also referred to as 'Godley's Own' or 'Godley's Incapables'.

H.W.B. Joseph of New College joined parades on Balliol cricket ground, and, on 8 October he marched with a company 'who marched out to a skirmish under Wytham Wood; but as we'd no umpire, it was only an exercise in scouting and taking cover'. The volunteers held one of their early field days near Witney when an ominously-named Red Army was intended to drive the White Army from its position. Unfortunately, the proceedings were 'considerably hampered by the

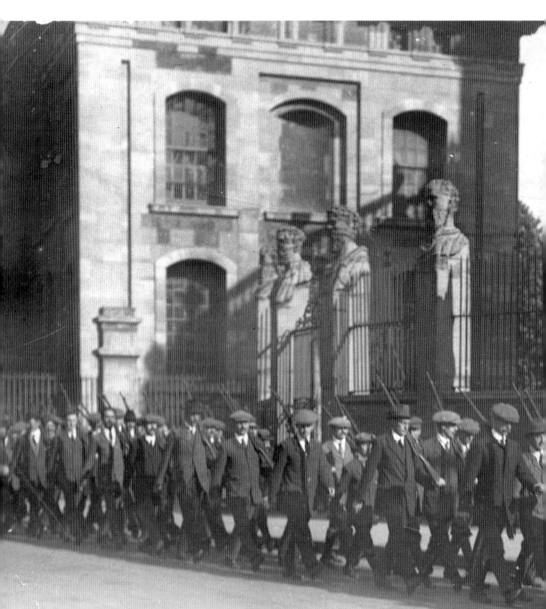

Men in the Oxford Volunteer Training Corps march past the Sheldonian Theatre, 1914. They were a home guard of older men, founded in August 1914 by A.D. Godley, the University's Public Orator. Known affectionately as 'Godley's Incapables', they paraded at first in civilian clothes.

number of sightseers, on cars, motor bicycles, and on foot', and the Chief Umpire decided that the Red Army had not attained its objective. By the end of 1914 volunteer forces were organised on a county basis and men were issued with uniforms, at first grey green, and eventually standard khaki after the War Office officially recognised them as soldiers at Easter 1916. Ultimately, the forces were assimilated into the military and Godley's Own became the 1st Volunteer Battalion Oxfordshire and Buckinghamshire Light Infantry in July 1918.

The War Office was equally slow to find useful work for the Volunteers, and local units only began shifting stores at the new Didcot Ordnance Depot in autumn 1915 following an appeal by the commandant. The national press gleefully imagined academics at work: 'Here might be seen a learned professor painting a bucket, while a renowned historian fearfully carried plates'. Godley had to admit that only a sprinkling of academics took part in these regular work parties.

The formation of a motor platoon in November 1915 was another local initiative, designed to provide a flexible response to an enemy invasion. Members of the Oxford Motor Volunteers included heads of houses, dons, undergraduates and Prince George of Teck. They paraded with their cars, and practised rifle-shooting and grenade-throwing as well as attending lectures on topics such as 'alternative fuels for motor traction'. In September 1917, a Heavy Transport Section for local lorry drivers was set up before the Army Council adopted the scheme nationally.

During the last eighteen months of the war, the Volunteer Corps provided initial military training for 17-18 year olds and cadet corps were established at some Oxford schools. Volunteers replaced regular soldiers by undertaking tasks such as patrolling lengths of railway line and guarding Leafield Wireless Station. In summer 1918 a service company was sent to the east coast for three months to guard against invasion, and as late as October, officers of the local Volunteer Battalions were called to a War Office meeting about a possible invasion at Deal. Within days home defence ceased to be a priority and members of the 1st Battalion were urged to return their arms and equipment in December; a parade was called for 2 January 1919 when men were to fill in trenches they had dug in New College cricket ground.

Parade of the Oxford Motor Volunteers in Davenant Road, March 1918. Motorcyclists and car drivers were urged to join this special section of the Oxfordshire Volunteer Regiment which was to provide a mobile response in the event of invasion.

Rumours of a Zeppelin raid in September 1914 saw Oxford plunged into gloom as street and shop lighting was reduced. This was a temporary scare, and full lighting was back on by November. Following the first German air raid on Britain on 19 January 1915, the Mayor published a notice warning Oxford citizens and colleges considered taking out insurance against air raid damage. In August 1915, the City Council turned off the principal electric street lights as an economy measure, and it took another Zeppelin scare before the council decided in October to obscure the tops of lights to hide them from the air and to turn off all but a few essential street lights

The Mayor of Oxford's air raid warning, January 1915. News of the first German bombing raid on England on 19 January 1915 swiftly led to these precautionary measures.

CITY OF OXFORD.

AERIAL RAIDS

Should hostile aircraft appear at Oxford the Brigadier General, General Staff, Southern Command, advises that the following precautions should be taken :—

1. Warning will be given to the inhabitants at the earliest possible moment by the sounding, for at least five minutes, of the hooter at the Great Western Railway Engine Works.

2. All lights should be immediately extinguished. The supply of gas and electric light will be cut off at the respective works. Consumers of gas should, for their own safety, turn off the gas, shut off the gas at the meters, and not turn it on again until the following morning. Inhabitants using other forms of light should at once pull down the blinds, and darken their houses.

3. All inhabitants and passengers in the streets should at once take refuge. The safest places are the cellars or the lowest rooms in each building.

W. E. SHERWOOD,

January 23, 1915. Mayor.

HOLYWELL PRESS, LTD., OXFORD.

at 11pm. Oxford was covered by a new Home Office Lighting Order in February 1916 which limited street lighting to those lamps judged necessary for public safety and introduced restrictions on private and shop lighting. Christ Church decided to silence Great Tom at night for

Oxford Volunteers parade on Balliol College cricket ground, 1914. The group includes the tall figure of Sir Walter Raleigh, Professor of English (second from right) and the Poet Laureate, Robert Bridges (third from right).

fear that someone in an airship might recognise the sound. Candles replaced electric light in the Hall at Magdalen College and the story went around that Oriel had given up using tablecloths because they might reflect even the candlelight.

The black-out soon led to accidents – a soldier, Private Robert Harris, was killed by a bus in dark St Margaret's Road – and to court cases as householders were accused of showing lights. Heinrich Germer, a hairdresser in King Edward Street, was the first person to be charged in April 1916, and the *Oxford Chronicle* felt obliged to stress that his loyalty and patriotism were not in doubt.

Elliston & Cavell advertised 'Darkening Blinds and Curtains' and the Mayor urged pedestrians to keep right on the pavements to avoid collisions. The *Oxford Times* commented in October 1916 on Oxford's 'rather unfortunate habit' of walking in the roadway. Soldiers were especially guilty, and 'the fact that khaki blends so exactly with the colour of the road makes it difficult at night to see a soldier even at a few yards.'

In Cowley the bases of street lamps were painted white as a precautionary measure, but, to the fury of some residents, fine trees in Banbury Road were felled in December 1917 because people were walking into them in the dark.

No enemy Zeppelins or aircraft ever reached Oxford, but Rachael Poole recalled that 'an amateur fire brigade, which included heads of colleges and their wives, was ready to rush, at the first signal of alarm, to surround the Bodleian Library lest help should be required.'

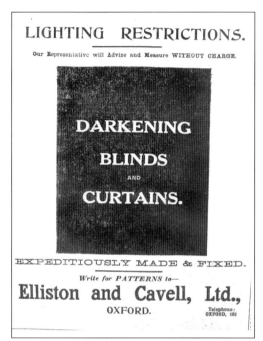

Expeditiously made and fixed black-out blinds and curtains, 1916. Elliston's advertisement followed the introduction of lighting restrictions, which even led to the Randolph Hotel being fined because a guest had left the light on when he fell asleep.

The GWR station hooter sounded the alarm several times during the war and brought a rush of special constables, soldiers from the

Volunteer Corps, Officer Cadets, Boy Scouts and St John's Ambulance personnel to pre-arranged positions. H.W.B. Joseph was disturbed in New College by an alarm at 11.30pm on 7 March 1916:

> 'I got up (having gone to bed and begun reading). Bugles were going everywhere, and the troops were patrolling, seeing that lights were extinguished, and people in their houses.'

In North Oxford, Isabel Dixey recorded in her diary: 'Last night Zeppelin night. Hooter at 1.5am. Altered M[aud]'s Tussore dress.' Colleges took air raid precautions seriously, and, in 1917, a notice in Brasenose College lodge advised: 'In case of air raids, the basement of no. XII is recommended for safety and warmth'.

When the alarm was heard at St Hilda's College, Joan Curzon recalled that 'we were made to get out of bed, put out any fires in our rooms, and descend to the then dining room with cushions where we found the Principal ready to entertain us by reading Kipling.' Although Oxford experienced only false alarms, air raids on London in 1917 brought a flurry of evacuees to the city. 'Watcher' in the *Oxford Chronicle* noted in October that trains from London had been 'quite packed' during the past week, especially with the 'well-to-do classes.' One of Oxford's leading hotels had had twenty or so people sleeping in the lounge and estate agents were receiving dozens of enquiries about furnished houses.

St Frideswide's Boys' School admitted several London boys at this time, including 'Edmund and Christian Dunkel from Leytonstone – Russian nationality, leaving London because of air raids'. Yiddish was heard in Oxford in March 1918 as raids brought another rush of Londoners, but local people expressed mounting impatience with continued lighting restrictions which *The Oxford Times* condemned as 'Prussianism triumphant in a democratic country'. Public street lighting was improved in autumn 1918, but, for shops, Morton's 1917 sale advertisement still applied: 'Inspect the windows in the day time as after screening time they have to be quite dark.'

Taking down the Kaiser's portrait in the Examination Schools as the building was being converted into a military hospital symbolised the abruptly changed relationship between Oxford and Germany in August 1914. The King of Prussia pub at Rose Hill quickly changed its name to the Allied Arms. There were rumours of German governesses travelling with bombs in their trunks, and Espionitis, the fear of spies, was everywhere.

The *Oxford Chronicle*, of September 1914 had a story about a suspicious carrier pigeon:

> 'It is reported on good authority that a carrier pigeon had been brought down near Oxford, that it was found to be conveying a message in German, and that it has been forwarded by the military authorities here to the War Office.'

The Oxford photographer, Henry Taunt, was twice reported to the police as he and his assistant went around the county on 'an extraordinary foreign-looking quadricycle'. C.P. Webber, the owner of Webber's store, had to deny that he was German and confirm that his family was Cornish. Lieutenant Colonel Raymond Schumacher, who had made a fortune in South Africa and was now the highly patriotic tenant of the Wytham estate, was granted a Royal licence to adopt his mother's maiden name, Ffennell, in 1916. William Sonnenschein, Vice-Principal of Brasenose College, thought it best in 1917 to take his paternal grandmother's surname, Stallybrass. Even music by German composers was liable to provoke hostility and Elspeth Baumann, a German girl stranded in Oxford, was 'discovered crouched over the music stool sobbing convulsively' after her piano playing was drowned out by 'Rule Britannia' from next door.

Hermann Fiedler, Taylorian Professor of German, had his allegiance to Britain called into question in *The Varsity* in February 1915 under the heading, 'Can the Leopard Change his Spots?' This prompted a public protest from 144 undergraduates 'against innuendo and veiled threats', and H.W.B. Joseph paid the Fiedlers a visit to stress his support. Fiedler subsequently wrote to the *Oxford Magazine* criticising the sinking of the *Lusitania* and the Germans' use of poison gas, and the petty persecution ceased.

F.C. Coneybeare, a leading Oxford scholar and theologian, caused huge controversy when his comment in a private letter that Sir Edward Grey had 'tricked' Britain into the war was made public. He refused to retract, and felt obliged to leave Oxford for Folkestone in 1917. Professor Sir Walter Raleigh came under attack in July 1918 after referring to German chivalry at a school speech day, but he retaliated

Belgian refugees at Ruskin College, September 1914. The plight of the refugees attracted great sympathy and an Oxford committee was formed to provide homes, work and schooling for them. Some older Belgian students were admitted to the University.

robustly, criticising the press for trying to make out that 'we are fighting orang-outangs' and for failing to tell the whole truth about our enemies' conduct.

Britain had gone to war in defence of Belgium and the country's soldiers and refugees were welcomed with open arms. Wounded Belgian soldiers were brought to the Third Southern General Hospital,and received so much attention that the editor of *The Varsity* feared it would become embarrassing. An Oxford Belgian Refugees' Committee was set up in September 1914 in association with the London Committee. Two committee members went to Folkestone and Alexandra Palace in London to choose refugees who were initially housed at Ruskin College and in large North Oxford houses.

War damage to the Universities of Louvain, Malines and Liège excited additional sympathy within the University, and about twenty Belgian refugees became unmatriculated undergraduates, with free accommodation in Oxford colleges. Some colleges also provided

Serbian refugees in Oxford, May 1916. These boys aged between 8 and 18 were initially housed at Wycliffe Hall, and around fifty remained in the city until the end of the war, living at St Andrew's Lodge in Linton Road.

houses for Belgian refugee families and St John's College made space available for a boys' school; Ursuline nuns taught the girls at their Oxford convent. An Anglo-Belgian lingerie business was established in September 1914 to employ some of the women refugees, and Belgian wood carvers helped to start a local toy-making industry which aimed to replace German toys. In November 1914 a Belgian Day raised £1,863, attracting support from rich and poor, and an appeal for clothing soon filled a warehouse loaned by B.H. Blackwell.

Lady Osler, wife of the Regius Professor of Medicine, exploited her American connections to secure £100 from a Bostonian and Lady Mary Murray obtained six cases of clothes from Philadelphia. Beneath the surface the refugees began to be a source of tension. Volunteers at the clothing warehouse nicknamed one woman the 'Flemish Vulture' because she was always there, claiming the best of everything. Some of the men housed at Ruskin proved rather too keen on drinking and playing cards and the committee decided in October 'to place families of a rather better class there' and only to take 'work-people' in future if they had jobs. Suitable families and educated refugees continued to arrive and the number of Belgian refugees in Oxford rose from more than 200 in October 1914 to 460 in February 1915. Additional houses were offered in Headington and Iffley, and some families were housed in licensed lodging-houses which were empty because of the war. Some male refugees found temporary work locally, particularly at the

University Press and at the Oxfordshire Steam Ploughing Co in Cowley; most women and girls worked at embroidery or went into service. A social club for Belgian refugees was opened in George Street premises vacated by the Oxford University Dramatic Society in November 1914. As refugees returned home or found work elsewhere, in many cases making munitions, the number in Oxford fell steadily to around 200 by April 1916 and 157 in January 1917. The boys' school in St John's College closed in autumn 1918, and, before large-scale repatriation began in January 1919, its pupils shared temporary premises at 62 St Giles' with around 200 Belgian boys who had spent the war in Malvern.

Serbia, like Belgium, was viewed as a small country facing a bullying aggressor, and the plight of Serbian refugees in early 1916 excited great sympathy in Britain. The appeal launched in Oxford in February stressed that 'the Serbians are in very sore straits. They need everything and not merely the "soldiers' comforts" and the little extras that we all love to send to our own people.' A Serbian Flag Day in March raised £412, and, during dimly-lit cocoa parties at St Hilda's College, 'proud knitters' worked on blankets for Serbian babies. Around 30,000 boys had been among the refugees who escaped across the mountains from Serbia into Albania, and some of the survivors were brought to England and France. The London Serbian Relief Fund took responsibility for 300 boys, and largely through the intervention of Sidney Ball, Fellow of St John's College, around half came to Oxford in April 1916, and were initially housed at Wycliffe Hall. Some were soon sent to other places but a nucleus of about fifty remained.

St Andrew's Lodge in Linton Road became a Serbian colony, visited in September 1917 by Prince and Princess Alexis of Serbia. Serbian schoolmasters were among the refugees and they taught the boys at a school in classrooms provided by Mansfield College. The boys later attended other Oxford schools, including Magdalen College School and St Edward's School, and around fifteen were admitted to the University as unmatriculated undergraduates. They received a thoroughly English education and Sir Arthur Evans even provided cricket equipment to the party cycling off to a summer camp in Wiltshire in 1917. Serbian influence also pervaded Oxford as the city celebrated Kossovo Day in June 1916 and St Sava's Day the following January. St John's College allowed Orthodox services to be held in the college chapel and St Stephen's House briefly became a Serbian theological college in January 1918.

Waging war on the Home Front involved coping with shortages and privations, and Oxford colleges were quick to make savings. On 4 August 1914, H.W.B. Joseph at New College 'ordered some economies in the dinner ... and told the gardener we must do without a bulb order. These are small things, but if you cannot do bigger you must do smaller.' In October the college's governing body agreed to serve the same dinner at High Table as at Low Table for the duration of the war and to reduce the table allowance by 2/- (10p). Balliol College decided in September 1914 that 'for the present only cold baths could be supplied, and that times and tariffs be left to the Junior Bursar'. Following the Royal example of abstinence, Oriel College resolved in April 1915 'that no beer, wine or spirits should be served at the Buttery

Women helping with the harvest at Barton Farm, Headington in September 1915. Land Girls became necessary in rural areas because so many agricultural labourers joined the forces, and U-boat attacks reduced food imports. Mrs G.H. Morrell trained milkmaids at her dairy in Headington Hill Hall.

or the Common Room during the war'.

Commodity shortages increased as the loss of agricultural workers and miners to the forces led to reduced supplies of food and coal. Imports of oil, paper, grain, sugar and other foodstuffs were hit by the German U-boat campaign. An Oxford Food and Thrift Week was held in July 1915 when Florence Petty, known unflatteringly as 'The Pudding Lady', discussed and demonstrated substitutes for meat, the making of bean pies, and the food value of different foods. An Oxfordshire War Agricultural Committee was appointed in October 1915 to increase food production, and there was a growing demand for allotment space in Oxford.

In 1915, Councillor B.H. Blackwell allowed unemployed men to grow potatoes on undeveloped land in Davenant Road, and he provided plots for volunteers organised by the Oxford Women's Service Committee in 1916. In December 1916, the Board of Agriculture empowered local allotment authorities to take over unused land for food production. Oxford City Council, prompted by Alderman J.R. Carter, soon created war allotments in every area of the city, providing 253 acres of allotments by May 1918, as against 104 in 1914. The Magdalen cricket ground in Cowley Road, the home of University cricket until 1880, was dug up in February 1917 and the Freemen of Oxford were persuaded to let part of Port Meadow be taken over for allotments in April. Christ Church allowed part of Merton Field to be converted into allotments which were cultivated, in part, by dons' wives and daughters and by nurses from the Third Southern General Hospital. In Botley Road, Corpus Christi College was compelled in 1918 to release grazing land west of Binsey Lane for allotments, and local demand for plots was so high that people took over land opposite that T.H. Kingerlee had raised for building and worked around the rubble.

Children at work on a war allotment in High Street, Headington, May 1918. Members of Headington Baptist Church had purchased this land near the church and were busy preparing it for cultivation.

Almost everyone became involved in food production – men, women, and children, undergraduates from the women's colleges, employees at Oxford University Press, Rhodes Scholars and Serbian refugees.

Food supplies continued to dwindle and long queues formed outside shops. May Cannan recalled butchers' closing in mid-morning – 'No beef, no mutton' – and grocers' shops sold out. Mrs Stone from Headington Quarry had to leave home at 6.45am three days a week, walk into the city, trudge from one queue to another, and finally return home at around 4pm. The distribution of food might also be unfair, and, in May 1917, a 94-year-old Oxford woman complained to the Mayor that 'we old folks of Oxford can't get a jot of sugar' whereas she had seen a lady allowed 5lbs with a large order. Rationing became necessary and Lord Devonport, the Food Controller, introduced a voluntary scheme in February 1917, seeking to restrict each individual to a weekly limit of 4lbs of bread, 2½lbs of meat and 4ozs of sugar; participating households could display a notice in their windows to prove their patriotism.

Women's colleges were quick to comply, and at Somerville there were soon complaints about unappetising food. Faced with boiled beetroot, a Swiss undergraduate was heard to ask: 'what ees this bloodee stuff?' Cadets in the men's colleges were at first exempt but they were being brought into the scheme by the end of 1917. The City Council appointed an Oxford Food Control Committee, including the Bursar of Oriel College, in August 1917 and compulsory sugar rationing of began in October; rationing was extended to butter and margarine in March 1918, and to meat in April. Guests could only be invited to dine in colleges on 'meatless' days, and a Christ Church don, J.G.C. Anderson, commented in July 1918: 'turnip soup...is food for cows and there is absolutely no need to serve such stuff. Haddock is a fish that needs far more skilful handling than the Ch Ch staff is capable of, to be palatable at all.'

The growing bureaucracy of food control in 1917-18 led to a maximum price for certain foods, including even tripe, and to the prosecution of Buol's restaurant for supplying a customer with too much cake at tea time. The production and sale of inessential products such as Banbury cakes and muffins was banned, and an old lady in Oxford who had a monopoly of making and supplying muffins had to

Women prepare food at the Jericho War Kitchen, February 1918. War kitchens were intended to save food and fuel and to provide cheap, wholesome food for those most affected by rising prices. The menu here included soup, meat and sausage rolls, and steamed lemon pudding.

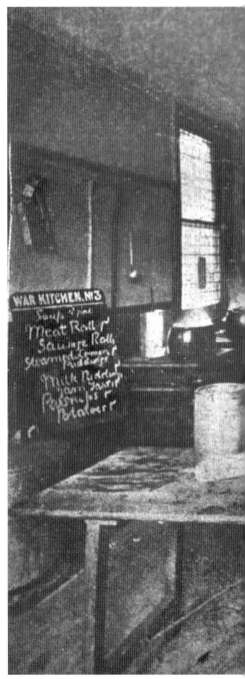

seek help from the City's Relief Committee in November 1917. Rising food prices and shortages most affected poorer people and the first communal kitchen was opened in March 1917. Oxford's first war kitchen was opened in a former Church Army Home in Cambridge Terrace in May and offered a midday meal daily except on Sundays. Up to 200 people a day were soon enjoying a typical menu of soup, meat and vegetable stew, treacle pudding and barley pancakes. A second war kitchen opened in Caroline Street, St Clement's in June, and a third in Canal Street, Jericho in February 1918. In May 1917 the War Kitchens Committee was asked to consider a war kitchen for North Oxford, which would not only save food and fuel, but also get round the shortage of domestic servants. The North Oxford National Kitchen eventually opened at 57/59 Woodstock Road on 31 December 1918, and its location suggests that it was primarily intended for rather less well-off households in the western portion of the suburb.

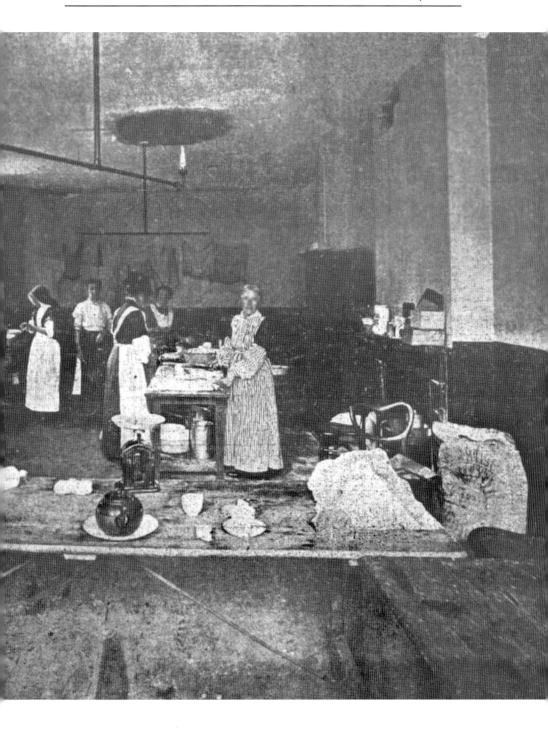

R 2.

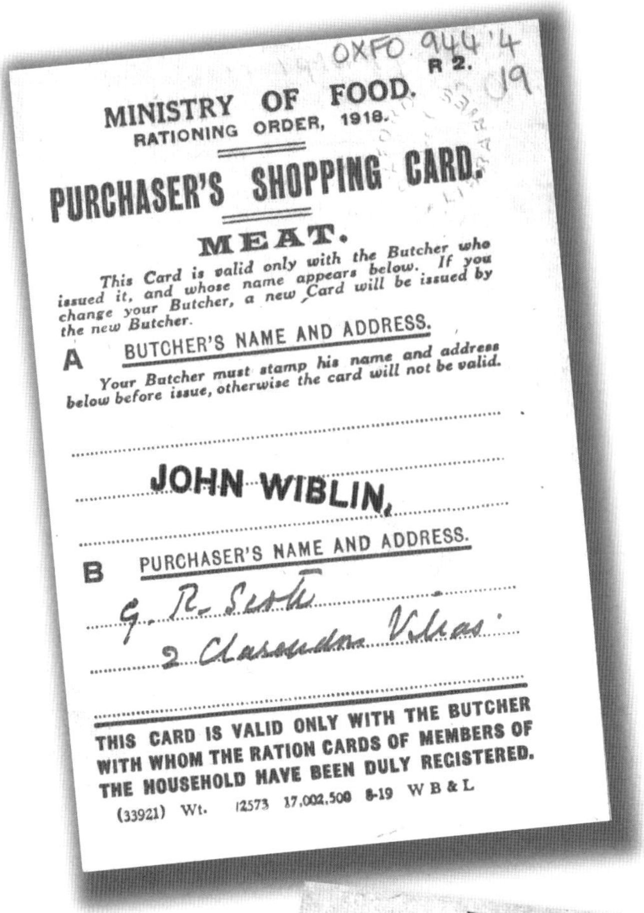

MINISTRY OF FOOD.
RATIONING ORDER, 1918.

PURCHASER'S SHOPPING CARD.

MEAT.

This Card is valid only with the Butcher who issued it, and whose name appears below. If you change your Butcher, a new Card will be issued by the new Butcher.

A BUTCHER'S NAME AND ADDRESS.

Your Butcher must stamp his name and address below before issue, otherwise the card will not be valid.

JOHN WIBLIN,

B PURCHASER'S NAME AND ADDRESS.

G. R. Scott
2 Clarendon Villas

THIS CARD IS VALID ONLY WITH THE BUTCHER WITH WHOM THE RATION CARDS OF MEMBERS OF THE HOUSEHOLD HAVE BEEN DULY REGISTERED.

(33921) Wt. 12573 17,002,500 8-19 W B & L

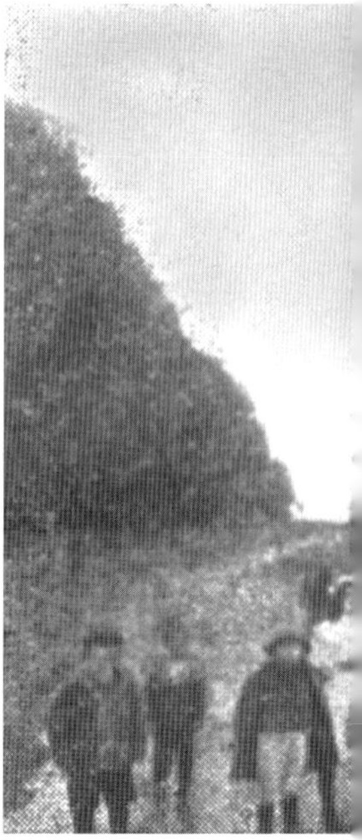

Ration cards issued to Oxford residents, 1918. Voluntary rationing failed to reduce food consumption sufficiently in 1917 and a compulsory scheme was introduced during 1918. The Ministry of Food card replaced the earlier Oxford Food Card issued to local photographer, Henry Minn.

FOOD CARD.
Oxford Food Control Committee. D. 3. Oxford

Customer's Name Henry Minn
Address 10 Leckford Rd Oxford

A, BUTTER AND MARGARINE.

B, TEA

1	2	3	4	5	6	7	8	9	10
11	12	13	14	15	16	17	18	19	20

C,

1	2	3	4	5	6	7	8	9	10
11	12	13	14	15	16	17	18	19	20

D.

1	2	3	4	5	6	7	8	9	10
11	12	13	14	15	16	17	18	19	20

CUSTOMER'S PART.

D.
Shopkeeper's Name:
Address:

C.
Shopkeeper's Name:
Address:

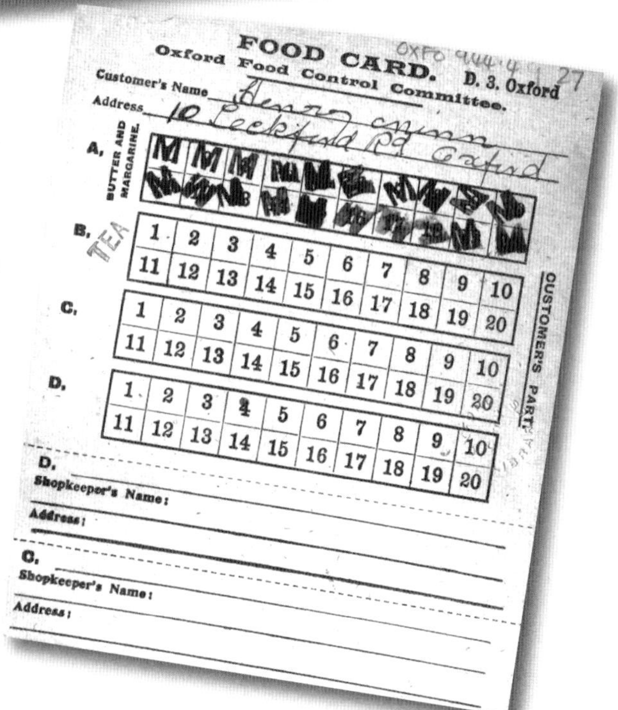

Queue outside Headington War kitchen in London Road, September 1918. Supported by the newly-formed Headington Women's Institute, this restaurant catered for both rich and poor and even attracted customers from Oxford who caught the bus up the hill.

In the meantime private enterprise aimed to capture the middle class market in November 1917 by opening a cooked food depot above St George's Café on the corner of Cornmarket and George Street. This offered ready-prepared dishes, cuts from joints, chicken, soups, fish pies, hotch-potch and vegetarian dishes, but amounts were restricted to rationing standards. A National Kitchen, supported by the newly-established Headington Women's Institute, opened in London Road in July 1918. This was designed for, and apparently used by, both rich and poor, and had a tasteful dining room with flowers as well as an upstairs room for children which workers could use if they wished. Oxford people came by bus for dinner and mothers living a mile away sent their children to fetch soup.

Other shortages added to the rigours of daily life in wartime. Bus services in Oxford were reduced as soon as the War Office requisitioned twelve of the Oxford Electric Tramway Company's

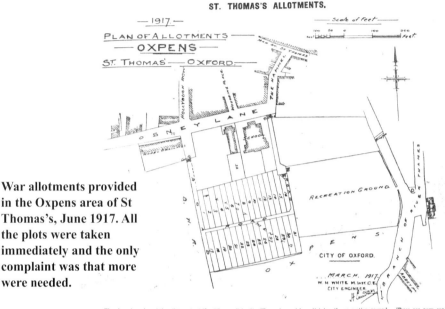

War allotments provided in the Oxpens area of St Thomas's, June 1917. All the plots were taken immediately and the only complaint was that more were needed.

Gas-powered bus during trials on the Stations and Cowley Road service, July 1917. Fuel shortages led to the introduction of gas buses in August and they were later used on other routes in the city.

twenty-eight buses in October 1914. Diminishing manpower and a reduced fuel allocation compounded the problems of both the company and intending passengers as the war continued. Rail cutbacks began in April 1915, when Oxford lost recently introduced suburban rail services on the Great Western Railway. Railway companies, suffering from wartime shortages of labour and rolling stock, tried to reduce passenger traffic by service reductions, fare increases and discouraging people from travelling. Somerville College undergraduates stayed on for a Vacation Term in July 1917 because of the difficulties of railway travel.

Coal shortages had an increasing impact later in the war leading to temporary closures at some local schools in early 1917; at Headington Quarry School in February the ink froze in the inkwells. Muriel Attlee recalled that at St Hilda's College the coal bunkers were kept locked. Each undergraduate was issued with a small bucket of coal for the evening and the sociable solution was for three or four women to pool their meagre supplies and work in one room. The Principal, Miss Burrows, insisted that undergraduates should wear evening dresses, without cardigans, at dinner and she was incredulous when Muriel presented a request to change this rule: 'With the men in the trenches dying and you just wanting to be better clothed.' She was unmoved by Muriel's reply: 'What good it will do the men in the trenches if we die of cold.'

At Oriel, the College Treasurer outlined living conditions in April 1918:

> 'I am today burning the gas stove at its lowest reducible point and have got rid of the use of the electric radiator ... I also sit in semi-darkness in the evening and we have abolished the lighting of the staircases.'

Following the Fuel and Lighting Order 1918 which aimed to cut the use of gas and electricity by one-sixth, the City Council appointed a Fuel Overseer. Most Oxford shops decided to close early at 6pm during the coming winter to save fuel. Gas and coal were rationed and, at Corpus Christi College, the governing body was told in November that the Coal Controller could not provide one allocation for the college and another for resident cadets. He would allow them 215½ tons altogether plus an allocation for baths.

The reduction in paper imports led to smaller, more expensive newspapers, and the *Oxford Chronicle* was only available to order from March 1917. Stores like Elliston's ceased to issue annual sale catalogues and at Cowley St John Boys' School, the headmaster, Herbert Tozer, reported in the summer 1918:

> 'Great difficulties in continuing the ordinary lessons in written work owing to the fact that only <u>scraps</u> of paper are available – as most exercise books are filled up and no new ones are at hand.'

Waste paper collections provided a partial solution to the crisis, and, by April 1917, Councillor Armstead and other helpers had organised a voluntary scheme with the support of local Boy Scouts. The City Council then appointed a By-Products Committee which extended the scheme across the city with a central depot on Christ Church premises in St Aldate's. Alderman Carter reported that schoolchildren were 'as keen as mustard' to become involved. They also took part in collections of horse chestnuts which replaced acetone from imported maize in the manufacture of cordite.

What did Oxford men on leave make of the city in wartime? They returned to a place which, on the surface at least, had scarcely changed. The buildings were undamaged, colleges appeared still to be functioning, shops were filled with goods, cafés were doing good business, and cinemas were becoming ever more palatial. Salter's steamers still plied the River Thames in summer, and although St Giles's Fair had been suspended, crowds still gathered on Magdalen Bridge on May Morning to hear the choir singing from Magdalen Tower. Small wonder that fellows on leave told a private in the 1/4th Ox and Bucks that it was 'hard to realise there was a war on.' There were reports of 'idle young fellows about Oxford' and complaints about the forward behaviour of young women. There was indeed a gulf between men in the trenches and the people back home who could scarcely begin to comprehend the conditions under which their loved ones lived and risked their lives on a daily basis. Soldiers found it difficult to cope with well-meaning sympathy and with views of the war that had been shaped by propaganda.

In reality, of course, the ever-lengthening casualty lists put everyone at home with serving relatives and friends under constant strain. In February 1915, Bessie Bryant, the table maid at the Rev Andrew Clark's Oxford hotel, told him that her sister had a husband who 'was at the war. They look at the *Oxford Journal* with terror every week; it has such a frightful weekly list of Oxford men killed.' One little family unit in Jericho was shattered in July 1916 as Private A.J. Rennie, serving with the 1/4th Ox and Bucks, was killed in France and the couple's baby died in a tragic scalding accident. A South Hinksey woman drowned herself in the Thames, and tried to drown her daughter, while her husband was serving at the front. One soldier's wife had children by two other men while he was away; another soldier secured custody of the children after his wife, a war worker, had an affair with her boss.

Society was disrupted by the war as Oxford found itself without its usual 3,000 male undergraduates and thousands of men of military age from the resident population. This made for a quieter city without the customary undergraduate misbehaviour and the University Proctors recorded strikingly few breaches of discipline during the war. Officer cadets had a more serious purpose, and most came straight from the trenches to Oxford for what Joanna Cannan described as their 'three months of cinemas and shops and shows and gramophones, one-steps and the girls, three months without night patrols, mud, duckboards, bully beef, vermin...' They did their best to keep up student traditions at the New Theatre, sitting stony-faced in the stalls during a comedy, and tearing sheets of calico to make a ripping noise while women dancers were high-kicking.

Prosecutions for drunkenness continued to fall from 144 in 1911 to eighty in 1914 and just fifteen in 1917 before rising again to forty-two in 1918. Breweries' output was limited and defence regulations restricted pub opening hours. It was an offence to supply wounded soldiers with alcoholic drink, and, in February 1916 for example, two married women, Rose Jackson and Daisy Ewers, were sentenced to a fine of 40s (£2) or a month in prison for attempting to buy whisky for men at the GWR station who proved to be hospital patients. In February 1918, Albert Thornton, licensee at the Queen's Arms in Park End Street, was fined £5 for selling a bottle of spirits to a wounded soldier. Prosecutions were rare, but this might have owed something to the reduced strength of the city police force. The Chief Constable admitted in 1916 that the regulation about treating wounded soldiers was frequently broken. Discussing licence renewals in St Ebbe's and Holy Trinity in March 1917, he reported that he had been forced to send in special patrols after receiving many complaints about women drinking with soldiers on leave and hospital patients having too much to drink. The Administrator of the Third Southern General Hospital had put the area out of bounds to patients and military police were also patrolling there.

Mrs A.L. Smith, wife of the Master of Balliol, attended the Licensing Sessions on behalf of local temperance organisations, arguing for more pub closures and drastic controls over the drink trade. She quoted an Australian cadet as saying: 'I have seen nothing in Sydney of drink and wickedness equal to what I have seen in Oxford.' Despite this plea, the licensing magistrates decided to close only five pubs, four of them in the St Ebbe's district. To provide a sociable alternative to the pub, temperance campaigners opened a non-alcoholic pub, the Three Feathers, in converted premises at 29-30 St Aldate's Street, in July 1916. This had a shop-restaurant and bathrooms on the ground floor with a dining room, a women's rest room and six bedrooms upstairs. It was designed particularly for women and girls, mothers who could sit in the garden and do their mending, bus conductresses after 'so much standing and jolting', and girls needing 'a clean dainty bedroom' at 1/6d (7½p) a night.

At a public meeting in the Sheldonian Theatre in March 1917 to promote a national campaign for social purity, the Rev R.W. Carew-Hunt wanted drastic steps to be taken against 'the undisguised harlotry of the streets'. There can be little doubt that the large-scale military presence in wartime Oxford proved highly attractive to young women deprived of male company.

An Oxford Vigilance Committee report on the Moral Condition of Oxford in November 1916 warned of the spread of immorality and described the central streets in the evenings as 'crowded with young girls, whose dress, and frivolous, not to say impertinent, behaviour show that they are deliberately laying themselves out to attract men.'

Concern about these 'flappers' prompted the introduction of

volunteer women patrols in Oxford before May 1916 to exert an element of moral control. They were described as 'a great restraining force, they had no legal authority, no power of arrest, and it required a great deal of tact to carry out the work successfully'. They attempted to deter the girls and move them along but they also noted and reported all instances of immorality. Patrols observed, for example, the activities of EF on the canal towpath north of Hythe Bridge. She would make arrangements with a man who would come to the site and rendezvous with a younger woman in the bushes while a man on the canal bridge kept a look-out for the police. The Vigilance Committee also worried that 'a large number of soldiers' wives encourage soldiers to visit them in their houses for immoral purposes'. The City Council was concerned enough about 'the number of women ... who required careful guarding' to employ two policewomen in 1917, unusually – and controversially – at a salary higher than that of police constables.

The true scale of the problem is again hard to quantify since

CHILDREN AT WAR

Children were soon playing soldiers and nurses as the streets of Oxford filled with uniformed men and women, bugles and military bands became familiar sounds, and armed sentries stood outside familiar buildings with a new wartime use. Tales of heroism by soldiers and sailors stimulated children's imaginations and British toy manufacturers introduced war games, models of the latest artillery pieces and even trench warfare systems with wire entanglements.

The war immediately affected children in the home as fathers, older brothers and other male relatives enlisted and they had to rely on field postcards and letters to keep in touch. They seemed likely to suffer financially as well because breadwinners left for the war and peace-time jobs were lost, but many households benefited as wives and mothers received separation allowances and women had more employment opportunities.

At school women teachers replaced men of military age and children became involved in the war effort through patriotic displays and fund-raising. They grew potatoes in school gardens, collected blackberries or horse chestnuts, and entertained wounded soldiers. Exercise books were rationed as paper became scarce and schools were forced to close when coal ran out. Girl Guides raised money by giving concerts, while Boy Scouts supported fund-raising events, delivered messages, and collected material for recycling.

There was of course a darker side to the war. The remaining adults had little time to look after and entertain their children and juvenile delinquency increased. Young girls were accused of flaunting themselves in front of soldiers. Most tragically, many fathers and brothers never came back, and in September 1915, Sergeant Percy Chapman of the 1/4th Battalion Ox and Bucks reported finding a 4-year-old girl's birthday party invitation on her father's temporary grave. It had arrived on the day he was killed.

the annual number of prosecutions for prostitution remained in single figures throughout the war. Reginald Thomas described casual sex with a barmaid from the Eagle and Child pub in a sentry box outside the Corn Exchange in George Street. In April 1918 a sexual encounter led to a married woman being charged under the defence regulations for passing venereal disease on to a cadet at Lincoln College. Two male doctors supported him, but, after evidence from Dr Helen Leyton, a bacteriologist, the case was dismissed. The illegitimacy rate in Oxford actually fell from 5.8 per cent in 1914 to 4.5 per cent in 1920, although the Vigilance Committee argued that abortions and 'forced marriages' were playing a part in this reduction. Venereal disease was certainly on the increase, and the Radcliffe Infirmary agreed to open a free treatment clinic in 1917, receiving 161 new patients in 1920.

The Q. O. OXFORD HUSSARS are "holding their own" at OXFORD

A soldier embraces a uniformed nurse in a postcard view that had been specially adapted for sale in Oxford. Romances blossomed in hospitals and billets and there was much official concern about the young women or 'flappers' who flocked into Oxford to meet recruits and convalescing soldiers.
Soldiers of Oxfordshire Trust

With fathers away in the services and mothers out at work, children's lives were disrupted and their increasing restlessness became a major concern. At St Frideswide's Boys' School in March 1917, the headmaster, Charles Wigg, punished a 12-year-old boy for truanting, lying and stealing from his mother. The boy's father was at the front and 'the mother seems to have let the boy get out of control'. In October 1918 magistrates sent another boy away for sleeping all night in railway carriages. Wigg had had to punish him frequently for lying, swearing, smoking, stealing and other grave faults. Herbert Tozer, at Cowley St John Boys' School, recorded an incident – clearly one of many – in March 1918 when youths climbed over the wall, vandalised the premises and badly damaged a teacher's bike.

In November 1916, Councillor Amos George blamed the rise in juvenile misconduct, hooliganism and misdemeanour on the loss of the most efficient trained teachers to the forces. The absence of male teachers meant fewer sporting opportunities for boys and there were fewer men to support Boy Scout troops and Boys' Clubs. Balliol Boys' Club in Littlegate Street managed to keep open, generally for three evenings a week, throughout the war but there were no boys' football leagues across the city in 1915-16. An initiative by the Board of Education in early 1917 aimed to tackle juvenile crime by establishing play centres; a Children's Happy Evening Association was formed in Oxford, chaired by Charlotte Green of 56 Woodstock Road. An Oxford Centre started in South Oxford School in March 1917, opened three short evenings a week, one for girls and two for boys. By May 1918 a permanent superintendent had been appointed and eight to ten lady helpers were needed to cope with the numbers of children attending.

Everyone needed distraction from the strains and stresses of war, and there was plenty of entertainment in Oxford, much of it staged to support good causes. Dr Hugh Allen, organist at New College, arranged a long series of Saturday evening popular concerts which migrated from the Corn Exchange to the Randolph Assembly Room and eventually, in February 1916, to the Holywell Music Room. In 1917 Dr Allen gave organ recitals at New College and organised a hymn-singing service at the Sheldonian Theatre in support of the Banbury Road VAD hospital. The Sheldonian, lit by electricity at the beginning of the war, provided a venue for major concerts featuring Clara Butt, the teenage pianist Solomon, and Moisewitch, the last one being in aid of the Radcliffe Infirmary. Ivor Novello was among the singers at an evening concert at Wadham College during Red Cross Day in June 1915. Less exalted concerts took place all over the city at venues as varied as the YMCA Hut at Cowley Barracks, Summertown Congregational Church and the temperance pub, the Three Feathers. Concert parties such as the Oxford Finches and the Hollyberries raised funds for many good causes.

The New Theatre, despite losing twenty-nine employees to the services, offered plays and entertainments throughout the war and

Wounded soldiers gather outside the Electra Cinema in Queen Street before seeing the Battle of the Somme film, September 1916. Cinema-going became hugely popular in wartime, and the Electra claimed to have entertained 27,000 wounded soldiers by March 1916.

THE BRITISH TOPICAL COMMITTEE FOR WAR FILMS
request the pleasure of the company of Bearer and Friend on
THURSDAY NEXT, AUGUST 10th, at 11.30 a.m. prompt,
when they will present
OFFICIAL PICTURES
of the
"BATTLE of the SOMME,"
Taken by Special Arrangement with the
WAR OFFICE
and under their direction.

No "Exclusive Rights" of this film will be granted.
Schedule of prices can be obtained from the sole booking director, W. F. JURY.

welcomed wounded soldiers free of charge to some performances. The Clarendon Press Institute was a regular venue for amateur music-making and drama from November 1915 as the entertainments committee sought to keep the club financially afloat in wartime and to raise money for comforts for Press men in the forces. Cinema-going became an increasingly popular activity. In 1916 Isabel Dixey recorded going to see Navy films at Walton Street, and '*What Became of Jones* to get a laugh'. Defending Edwin Fathers, chief projectionist at the Queen Street cinema, against conscription in March 1916, the manager, Mr Berry, reported that the cinema had entertained 27,000 wounded soldiers free of charge since the outbreak of war.

Many more attended the cinema in September when the official film, *The Battle of the Somme*, was screened. One man had recently had a leg amputated at the Third Southern General Hospital so the Administrator, Colonel Ranking, called in to check that he was all right. Cinemas were refurbished to add to their appeal; the Palace in Cowley Road reopened after major alterations in August 1917 with an orchestra accompanying the films. An organ and a second floor café lounge were soon added and the cinema was offering *Peter Pan*, 'one of the most elaborate films ever screened', in January 1918.

After the Government decided to close national museums as an economy measure in 1916, Dr Percy Gardner wrote to *The Times* pointing out that wounded soldiers accounted for a large proportion of the visitors to the Ashmolean Museum, and asking: 'are we to force them to the picture palace and the public house?' Oxford University decided to keep its museums open 'as humanising institutions, never more needed than at the present time'.

Outdoor sport for men virtually ceased during the war and drilling and entrenching took the place of most games in the University Parks. Some college cricket grounds were used as grazing land or taken over by the military while the unused Magdalen Ground became war allotments. Military football teams played at Oxford City's White House ground in 1915-16, and officer cadets took up cricket, rugby and athletics from 1916, holding sports days on the University track in

Soldiers' football final at Oxford City's White House ground in Abingdon Road, January 1916. Ox and Bucks Territorials on the attack during their 3-2 win over the 346th Army Service Corps XI.

Iffley Road. They also played golf, securing reluctant permission to play at the Cowley course on Sundays at the end of 1917. Rachael Poole noticed that parties of all kinds vanished from University life at an early stage, along with dinners and 'at homes'. Despite all the privations and the black-out, Margaret Verini, an undergraduate at St Hilda's College, recalled that 'Oxford was not sombre – we were young, we made bandages, dug, grew vegetables on the allotment'.

Popular songs kept people's spirits up and spawned imitations like *Dipperary*, a version of the quintessential wartime song *Tipperary* compiled by women training to be teachers at Cherwell Hall:

'It's a hard thing to be a teacher, it's a hard thing to train,
It's a bad thing for your temper, and a tax upon your brain.
Goodbye jeunesse dorée! Farewell feminine charm!
It's a hard, hard thing to be a teacher, A full-fledged school-marm.'

Chapter 6

Coming Home

NEWS OF BULGARIA'S SURRENDER on 30 September 1918 was flashed on the screens at the Queen Street and George Street cinemas drawing rounds of applause from the audiences. The long-awaited Armistice with Germany was announced more traditionally at around 11am on Monday, 11 November as a flag was hoisted on the turret of the General Post Office in St Aldate's amidst uproarious cheers. Most Oxford people became aware of the news as the bell Great Tom boomed out across the city from Christ Church.

Long before noon the colours of Britain and all the Allies were displayed throughout the city centre and impromptu bands using whistles, toys, spoons, combs and biscuit tins as instruments brought a carnival atmosphere to the streets. Officer cadets hurried to Carfax in their hundreds as lectures ended. Wounded soldiers poured in from military hospitals some in wheelchairs, attended by nurses, while others arrived by bus and scrambled out of the windows to save time. A small boy conducted a group of wounded soldiers along High Street, barking out orders like a sergeant major, while his companion beat time with a battered tin.

Margot Collinson and other St Hilda's College students abandoned work in the Radcliffe Camera and 'swarmed into the High and the Corn. I don't think any of us quite believed in it. I know I didn't. The undergrads relieved the situation. They got hold of an enormous motor lorry and careered around the town on it yelling and waving flags.' Another group of undergraduates hired a four-wheeler: 'One perched himself on the horse, and another, standing inside the vehicle, tried to play the bagpipes, the noise of which was happily drowned by the ringing cheers.'

The Carfax Copper found himself at the centre of a ring of whirling dancers and the Emperors' heads outside the Sheldonian Theatre were daubed with red paint during an afternoon noted 'for the general good order and remarkable good temper of the crowds'. Women students from St Hilda's were out again after lunch, processing around Oxford with the gong and the hall banner.

> 'All the third year had ridiculous tin trumpets and the rest of the band was provided by combs, etc., including Jacynth with a poker and shovel. We got ringed round by the Balliol men and some of the Hertford cadets, which was great fun.'

The Mayor read the terms of the Armistice to a crowd of several thousand people at Carfax at 6pm and an effigy of the Kaiser was burned on the bonfire at a firework display in St Giles' in the evening. Margot Collinson and her friends were out again:

> 'We had to go in twos – neither more nor less – to enjoy the fun. The bonfire was just outside St John's, and all the time they sent up rocket signals, and aireoplane (sic) lights. So imagine St John's lit up in front by the lurid glare of the bonfire, and behind by the brilliant Ver[e]y lights – it was a gorgeous effect!'

The Oxford coal merchants, Stevens & Co., who had always commented about the progress of the war in their advertisements, now concluded the series with the rousing statement: 'The long struggle between the forces of enlightenment and the powers of darkness is virtually ended, and, RIGHT has triumphed over MIGHT.'

The Armistice was celebrated too in Oxford colleges. At Magdalen the President, Sir Herbert Warren, ordered the college bells to be rung as soon as the bell-ringers could be assembled and celebratory peals rang out across

Right triumphs over Might, a celebratory advertisement by coal merchants, Stevens & Co., at the end of the war. This was the last of a long series of adverts promoting the sale of their coal and commenting about the progress of the war.

the city during the afternoon of 11 November. At dinner that evening, the depleted academic body – President, Fellows and undergraduates – occupied the high table while officer cadets filled the body of the hall. At New College, Warden Spooner spoke after dinner in hall and everyone present, members of the college, officers, cadets, their serving staff and college servants drank a toast to the King's health. Corks popped in Oriel College as the Armistice brought to an end not only the war but also the long period of official abstinence since the college had followed the King's lead in 1915. At St Hilda's College that evening, Frances Wintersgill recalled that the Bursar gave the students claret cup at dinner, an unheard of treat.

The sense of loss was all too obvious, however, and, at New College, H.W.B. Joseph 'felt as ready to weep as to cheer.' Mildred Macan, wife of the Master of University College, who had lost her son, Basil, in June 1915, wrote in her diary for Armistice Day:

> 'Most momentous day. Revolution growing in Germany, Kaiser fled to Holland, our progress quickening at the front ... later in the morning we heard the armistice was signed. It is hardly possible to fathom the relief. The town was all beflagged. Missed Basil somehow peculiarly.'

There were mixed feelings in the services, too, as the Armistice took effect. Adrian Keith-Falconer tried to summarise the emotions of men in the Oxfordshire Hussars as the guns fell silent at last:

> 'Officers and men were very tired, and little inclined either for wild excitement or deep reflection. They felt pride in victory, perhaps, when they thought about it; but yet more they felt relief and relaxation after great strain, quietly thankful that it was all over.'

For most men, demobilization became the main topic of conversation, but it could be a lengthy process. The Oxfordshire Hussars marched towards the River Rhine on 17 November before new orders sent them to winter quarters in the Ardennes. A few men were demobbed before Christmas but most had to wait until the end of January 1919. Demobilization from the Ox and Bucks was delayed for many men as battalions were deployed elsewhere. The 1st Battalion began to demobilize on the Euphrates early in 1919, but having returned to Aldershot in April, it was then reinforced and sent off with a relief force

CITY OF OXFORD.

HOME-COMING

OF THE

1/4 BATT. OF THE OXFORDSHIRE

LIGHT INFANTRY.

THE BATTALION WILL ARRIVE AT OXFORD

TO-DAY, MARCH 31,

at 2.54 p.m.,

and will be met by the Mayor and Corporation.
They will march to the Barracks preceded by the Oxford
Volunteer Band and the Volunteer Regiment will line the
Street.

ALL OFFICERS AND MEN who have served in the Battalion
during the present War are invited to parade at the G.W.R.
Station, thirty minutes before the time announced for arrival.
CITIZENS are invited to give our Oxford men a hearty
welcome on their return home.

LET THE FLAGS BE FLOWN

ON THE LINE OF MARCH.

ROBERT BUCKELL, Mayor.

HOLYWELL PRESS, OXFORD.

Returning men of the 2nd
Battalion Ox and Bucks leave the
'down' platform of the GWR
station on their way to Cowley
Barracks, 12 June 1919. The little
building in the background was a
cabmen's hut providing them
with shelter and the opportunity
for a hot drink between fares.

Let the Flags Be
Flown, 31 March 1919.
The Mayor urges
Oxford citizens to help
celebrate the precisely
timed home-coming of
members of the 1/4th
Battalion Ox and
Bucks.

to North Russia. The 2nd Battalion became part of the Army of Occupation, crossing over into Germany on 9 December as the band played the marches of the 43rd and 52nd Regiments. In March 1919 the 2/4th Battalion was re-constituted for service in Palestine, while the 3rd was sent to Ireland. The 7th and 8th Battalions spent the winter of 1918-19 in Bulgaria and men with longer war service were demobbed from there before the rest were sent to Egypt in April 1919.

Delayed demobilization was not only a problem for the individual, and, in February 1919, the Vice-Chancellor, Dr Blakiston, wrote to War Office stressing 'the enormous inconvenience... caused in many colleges by the absence of porters, scouts, and all manner of servants. It is bad enough to be without half the tutors, but the undergraduates mind this less than the absence of the servants.' Since servicemen returned to Oxford over a long period there were few opportunities to provide official receptions. The Mayor, Sir Robert Buckell, and city councillors gathered at Oxford's GWR station on 31 March 1919 to welcome home a unit, comprising forty-four men and four officers from the 1/4th Battalion Ox and Bucks, which had returned from service in Italy. The soldiers then marched to Cowley Barracks behind the battalion's band. Huge crowds watched from every possible vantage point along the route and the bells at Carfax Tower and All Saints' Church rang out as they passed. A unit of the 2nd Battalion had a similar reception in June, but around thirty men of the 132nd Oxfordshire Heavy Battery returned unexpectedly and without ceremony at the LNWR station on 26 May.

A smoking concert for 250 former members of the Oxfordshire Heavy Batteries was held at the Town Hall at the end of June. Oxford University Museum staff held a welcome home party for sixteen employees returning from war service in April 1919 where entertainments included ping-pong, quoits, skittles and 'an electric induction coil' to provide extra vitality. The Chairman, Mr Robinson, thanked the men 'for the sacrifices they had undergone during the long period of this terrible war'. At Christmas 1918, Oxford University Press sent a printed thank you to Private H.C. Harris and other serving employees, for 'your splendid services which have assisted in bringing the war to such a successful issue giving us Victory over our enemies and, we hope, Peace to the whole world.' In April 1919, 162 men were

Military celebrities outnumber other recipients of honorary degrees on Encaenia Day, 25 June 1919. The group includes, from left to right: back row, Henri Pirenne, Rear Admiral Sir William Hall, J.R. Clynes MP, Lord Robert Cecil; front row, Admiral Sir Rosslyn Wemyss, Lieutenant General Sir John Monash, General John Pershing, Marshal Joseph Joffre, Lord Curzon, Chancellor of the University, Field Marshal Sir Douglas Haig, Admiral Sir David Beatty, Herbert Hoover, General Sir Henry Wilson.

still in the forces and it was not until 19 September that a dinner and welcome home party was held for returned staff at the Clarendon Press Institute.

Both city and university publicly honoured men who had made major contributions to victory. On 3 February 1919 Admiral Sir Reginald Tyrwhitt was made an honorary freeman of the city at a well-attended ceremony in the Town Hall. The next day, he was awarded an honorary Doctorate of Civil Law at the Sheldonian Theatre and the

Public Orator, A.D. Godley, remarked that 'Oxford shone with the reflected glory of his achievements'. At the Encaenia ceremony on 25 June 1919 the University awarded honorary doctorates to military celebrities from the Allied nations, including Field Marshall Sir Douglas Haig, Admiral Sir David Beatty, Marshall Joseph Joffre, and General John Pershing. Not to be outdone, the City Council had a triumphal arch erected at Carfax and awarded the freedom of the city to Haig and Beatty in appreciation of their services to the British Empire during the war.

On 3 December 1918 the War Department wrote to the Vice-Chancellor, Dr Blakiston, listing no fewer than forty-one University and College

Admiral Sir Reginald Tyrwhitt.

premises it occupied and seeking a ranking order of need for their return to normal use. This was an impossible request in the Oxford context, but the Vice-Chancellor advised Colonel Ranking, Administrator of the Third Southern General Hospital, on 7 December that the University 'can easily do without the Examination Schools for the first half of 1919; less easily for Michaelmas Term 1919'.

In fact, student numbers rose much more quickly than anticipated as over 1,800 ex-servicemen matriculated or resumed their university careers in the first year after the war. One college was said to have freshmen of every military rank from lieutenant to lieutenant colonel. At Balliol College the departure of the last contingent of 150 officer cadets on 9 January 1919 was followed a week later by the arrival of the same number of undergraduates. The college had 160 undergraduates in residence, rising to 233 in Trinity Term and overcrowding led to the establishment of 'colonies' in Beaumont Street and Holywell Street. At Oriel the number of undergraduates rose to fifty-two in Hilary Term 1919 after the last RAF officers left and the college was soon eager to end Somerville's occupation of St Mary Hall quad.

The close proximity of male and female students, separated only by bricked-up passages, led on 19 June 1919 to the infamous 'Oriel Raid' when inebriated men, celebrating success on the river during Eights' Week, tried to break through to the women's quarters. On a warm night some of the women students had brought their bedding out into the quad and the noise sent them quickly back to their rooms. Classics don Miss Hilda Lorimer, wearing a 'hat with pendant ostrich feather', appeared in the quad and routed the revellers with the words: 'Gentlemen, have the courtesy to return to your own quarters without delay'. The Somerville College Principal, Miss Emily Penrose, set up a rota for guard duty at the breach in the wall and took the first watch herself, sitting in an armchair with a cup of coffee. Some accounts of the event have the Rev L.R. Phelps, Provost of Oriel College, sitting at the other side and he was clearly very upset by the episode. He wrote to Miss Penrose the following day, trusting that she 'will forgive and forget the outrage, for it is nothing less'. For her part she readily accepted that the incident was 'the thoughtless action of a few individuals'.

The War Office agreed to pay £2,050 towards reinstating Somerville College buildings in July 1919, and the college was able to return home for Michaelmas Term 1919. Both the cost and the time lag reflect the scale of the challenge which the authorities faced in running down local military hospitals. The various outposts of the Third Southern General Hospital had around 3,000 beds at the end of the war and the Ashhurst War Hospital in Littlemore was still growing towards its full capacity of 550 shell-shocked patients in September 1918. Probably the last Red Cross Ambulance train, carrying 100 patients, arrived in Oxford on 19 December and the numbers of in-patients began to decline. The military evacuated the Town Hall in December and came under pressure to leave Merton and University Colleges in the New Year. The last patients were removed from the Examination Schools in May 1919 and work could begin reinstating the building for its peacetime use.

Outside the city centre the Wingfield and Cowley Road hospitals became a separate orthopaedic unit in February 1919. The number of orthopaedic beds had risen steeply from 100 to 700 since 1917 and convalescing patients now had a choice of curative workshops and outdoor work on both sites. Gramophones played in the wards at Cowley Road and a 'wet' canteen opened in May 1919. In July, there was a sports' day which included crutch races, a tug of war between teams of nurses and a pillow fight between Captain Girdlestone and Captain Strange, both men sitting astride a pole. The Cowley Road site soon reverted to its pre-war role as Oxford Workhouse, but the Ministry of Pensions took over the Wingfield as an orthopaedic hospital for discharged soldiers. The Wingfield Committee stipulated that twenty-two beds should be reserved for children and the arrival of a first group on 20 November 1919 marked the beginning of the hospital's development under Girdlestone's guidance as a regional orthopaedic centre.

A similarly positive regime was in place at the Ashhurst War Hospital where Lieutenant Colonel Saxby Good, a neurologist attached to the Third Southern General Hospital, aimed to provide shell-shocked patients with 'a judicious mixture of work and play'. The refurbished asylum was described as providing airy dormitories, and cheerful day rooms with comfortable chairs. A YMCA hut soon provided recreational facilities in the grounds, and Good anticipated entertainments, organised games and even a cinema. The Ministry of Pensions took over the hospital in 1920 for the treatment of cases of neurasthenia, or nervous exhaustion, among discharged soldiers. Two years later it reopened as Littlemore Hospital, not as Littlemore Asylum, with Dr Good as enlightened Superintendent until 1937.

The future of discharged servicemen had become a major concern in Oxford as elsewhere during the war. In May 1915, local firms such as Cape's, Elliston's, Minty's, and Webber's signed up to a *Daily Telegraph* campaign, promising post-war to give preference to servicemen when filling posts. The Morris works at Cowley was already employing twenty-one discharged soldiers in January 1917, and thirteen former soldiers were driving buses for the Oxford Tramway Co in March. Some provision for disabled ex-servicemen was made through national appeals for Lord Roberts' Memorial Workshops and St Dunstan's. Locally, the Oxford Orthopaedic Centre provided workshops for training hospital patients in many trades from 1917. In addition the City Council's Pensions Committee opened a workshop at 30 St Aldate's in September 1918 to give disabled soldiers and sailors work in the boot-making and repairing trades.

Individuals sometimes attracted particular attention, and Charles Blackwell, a former private in the 5th Royal Irish Lancers who had been badly injured at Hooge, was presented with a hand-propelled tricycle in 1916 to enable him to travel around as a cleaner and repairer of typewriters.

After the Armistice finding jobs for the increasing number of discharged and disabled ex-servicemen became a greater challenge and the local Employment Exchange set up a special section headed by a former sergeant in the Ox and Bucks who had himself lost an arm in the war. Although some discharged men were able to return to their former jobs, 665 fit and 52 disabled ex-servicemen were still out of work at the end of 1920. The City Council organised relief work for the unemployed, including, in 1923, the building of the High Bridge over the River Cherwell in the University Parks and the widening of Botley Road.

Bertha Johnson, Principal of the Society of Home Students, urged women in 1918 to show 'their true patriotism' by turning away from war work 'to other work of national importance, such as teaching,

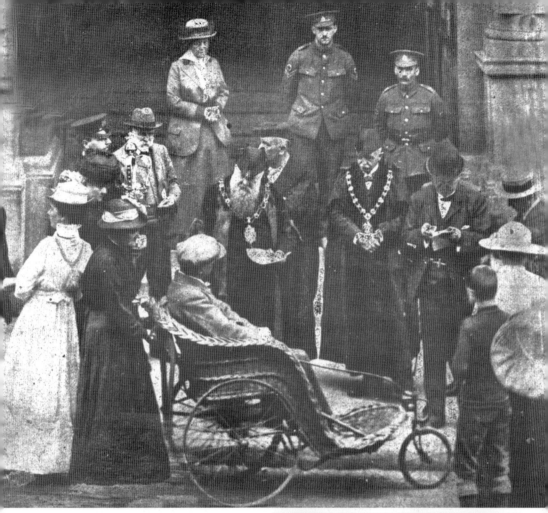

Charles Blackwell receives a hand-propelled tricycle from the Mayor of Oxford, Councillor C.M. Vincent, August 1916. A former private in the 5th Royal Irish Lancers, Blackwell was disabled following serious injuries at Hooge in 1915.

although their occupations may mean less novelty and possibly more drudgery'. Many women had undertaken war work, paid or unpaid, out of a sense of duty and they had no wish to continue it in peace-time. In many cases women had replaced enlisted men and they

Men building the High Bridge over the River Cherwell in the University Parks, 1923. Unemployment, especially among ex-servicemen, was a problem in Oxford after the war and this bridge was one of a number of public works intended to provide useful work.

would have anticipated losing their temporary jobs once the war ended. Other work generated by the war, in munitions factories or social clubs, for example, soon ceased. Willingly or not, many women returned to the home but there were some areas such as teaching, local government and retail where wartime changes proved to be more permanent.

At Oxford University women students soon found themselves outnumbered again. Ina Brooksbank, at St Hugh's College, wrote in February 1919:

'There are now half the number of men back, 1,500 and they are still coming. The history lectures are crowded out. They now have 100 men, where they used to have about five and twenty women ... Lots of the male coaches have refused to coach women any longer, and next they will turn us out of lectures if they get any more crowded ... They were glad enough to have us when they had no one else.'

Women had enjoyed a greater prominence in wartime Oxford, however, and few people now openly opposed the idea of granting them degrees and accepting them as members of Congregation. The reform of the parliamentary franchise in 1918, giving the vote to women at the age of 30, also helped those wishing to see women admitted to full membership of the University. The 'Women's Statute' was passed without significant opposition in February 1920 and the first women took their degrees in October 1920.

Wartime privations did not end with the Armistice. Public street lighting was partially restored in October 1918 and new incandescent lamps brightened the High Street. After 11 November the black-out was over at last enabling streets, shops, homes and colleges to be fully lit again for the first time since 1916. Indoors, however, the shortage of coal continued to create decidedly Spartan conditions. The Treasurer at Oriel College warned undergraduates in November that the Coal Controller was only allowing them a hundredweight sack a fortnight each, considerably less than current consumption. At Corpus Christi College freezing undergraduates

Women workers stitch car seats at the Morris Motors factory in Cowley in the 1920s. Local employment opportunities for women and girls quickly diminished at the end of the war, but there were still jobs in Oxford's growing motor industry.

strived to 'attain the cool heights of philosophical speculation... [while] struggling like so many puppies in a basket for a glimpse of the fire'. Only the timely arrival of logs seems to have averted threats to burn the furniture to keep warm. Limits on gas consumption forced Balliol College in February 1919 'to prohibit the service of hot eatables for tea in College during the present term.' Rationing of meat, butter and sugar under the Ministry of Food's Rationing Order 1918 continued until the beginning of 1920.

Increased concern for the health of the nation was an important outcome of the war. It reflected in part the high numbers of men judged to be medically unfit for military service and also the appalling infant mortality rates which considerably exceeded war losses. In July 1917 Sir William Osler insisted that, given good healthy mothers and good healthy homes, at least fifty per cent of the 100,000 babies lost each year could be saved. Wartime surveys exposed poor sanitary arrangements in many houses and 'one daintily dressed lady was greatly concerned for the children, whom she declared she found clothed chiefly in dirt'.

Long-term pressure on beds at the Radcliffe led to the acquisition of the Headington Manor estate in 1917, where the Osler Pavilion for tuberculosis patients was opened in 1927 – and the John Radcliffe Hospital in the 1970s. There were calls for new houses for the poor and for playing fields, but, when the Local Government Board asked the City Council to assess Oxford's post-war housing needs in 1917, it decided that 100 would be sufficient. This assessment was immediately condemned as inadequate, and Oxford went on to build 223 houses under the Housing Act 1919, most of them in Cowley Road, Iffley Road and Cumberland Road.

Once the war was over, Vera Brittain noted, 'Almost

Homes for Heroes at the so-called White City in Cowley Road, 1921. Designed in a cottage style by the Oxford Panel of Architects, these council houses were among the first built in the city following the Housing Act of 1919. Ex-servicemen and their families were preferred as tenants.

HEALTHY BABIES

National Baby Week in July 1917 took place in the context of the enormous loss of life during the war and the realisation that the country needed a growing, healthy population. Volunteer health visitors with the Oxford Health and Housing Association and earlier organisations had worked across the city since 1904 and claimed to have halved the local death rate among infants to 63 per 1000 by 1916. Nationally, Mrs Alys Russell informed the association in May 1915 that 200,000 babies a year were dying before and after birth compared with 150,000 men killed or injured during the first nine months of the war.

By July 1917 there were eight mother and baby welfare centres across the city and the City Council had appointed an infant welfare adviser, Sister Spencer. National Baby Week was marked by special sermons in city churches and advice was given to children in girls' schools. Three hundred mothers who had taken their children to be weighed regularly were invited to a baby show in Balliol College Garden Quad where the Mayor, Alderman Sir Robert Buckell, spoke briefly and they were all photographed on the steps of the Hall.

They also attended a special showing of a film *Motherhood* at the George Street Cinema where Sir William Osler, Regius Professor of Medicine, insisted that the country needed healthy mothers in healthy homes. He suggested the introduction of tribunals for bachelors aged 25, giving them just six months to get married!

In October 1917, a means-tested scheme was introduced to part fund the cost of milk for children under four, and the Radcliffe Infirmary decided in October 1918 to set up a maternity department. When it opened in July 1921, the Rev G.B. Cronshaw described it as 'payment of a long debt that Oxford owed to women'

immediately, Oxford became abnormally normal'. The University and Colleges were soon restored to their pre-war appearance, but conditions were different. Harold Macmillan could not bear to return and finish his degree: 'I just could not face it. To me it was a city of ghosts.'

Wartime inflation had reduced the value of college property and encouraged the sale of land which, in the local context, influenced the future development of Oxford. The war had created new links between the University and the state, and the University lost some of its independence in the 1920s when financial difficulties forced it to accept a Government grant. At the same time the war had enhanced the international standing of the University, particularly among the Allied nations, and Chairs of French and Italian were established. The opening of colleges to refugee students, officer cadet battalions, hospital patients, and disabled soldiers created a host of informal links across the globe. Some Oxford academics stirred huge controversy in October 1920 by holding out an olive branch to

The first women receive their degrees in the Sheldonian Theatre, October 1920. Women were largely responsible for maintaining academic life during the war, and opposition to making them full members of the University simply melted away in Oxford, if not in Cambridge.

German intellectuals. German Rhodes Scholars were eventually re-admitted to Oxford in 1929 and Hermann Fiedler continued as Professor of German until 1937, leaving a department which was described as 'a model for other universities'. Differing opinions about the war in Oxford led ultimately to the famous King and Country debate at the Oxford Union in 1933 which voted against shrill patriotism.

Some wartime changes had a lasting impact – for example, restricted pub opening hours, shorter shop hours, many more allotments, British Summer Time and the use of banknotes instead of gold coins. The language of war soon intruded into everyday speech, and, in May 1915, Miss Penrose, Principal of Somerville College warned her exiled students to be on their best behaviour at Oriel:

'We have, as it were, to defend against would-be critics a long line of trenches; each student has her bit of the line to keep. If a single student is exposed to the enemy, it will not mean merely a single casualty, but a gap in our line through which the critics will rush, will exaggerate and multiply.'

For the future of Oxford, the most significant change was the boost which the war delivered to industrial development at Cowley. Contemporaries were still entirely unaware of Cowley's potential, and the editor of the *Oxford Chronicle*, gazing into 1919, advised readers: 'the fact remains that the University is the citizens' greatest asset, and the activities which the University carries on are the only large industry that is ever likely to be established in Oxford.' In similar vein, the city's

Medical Officer of Health, A.L. Ormerod, noted that 'no new industries have arisen which are likely to have any marked effect on the population'. With a workforce of 200 in 1919, Morris Motors produced just 387 cars; by 1924, 5,550 employees were turning out 32,918 cars.

Edward, Prince of Wales, meets Edward Brooks VC, during a tour of the Morris Motors factory in May 1927. Like so many other ex-servicemen in the Oxford area, the former Company Sergeant Major and war hero found work in the burgeoning motor industry at Cowley.

Postscript

THE GREAT WAR was quite unprecedented in terms of the number of combatants and casualties. Great Britain mobilized around five million men during the war, France nearly eight million, Russia almost sixteen million, Germany thirteen million, and Austria-Hungary nine million. Around twelve per cent of these men – one in eight – were killed in the war, and Britain lost over 750,000 men.

The Ox and Bucks lost 5,878 officers and men during the conflict. Of the 14,792 University men who served in the forces, 2,716 (18.36 per cent) died. For some colleges, the proportion of casualties was even higher. At Balliol, 183 (twenty-two per cent) of the 838 men serving in the British forces were killed; at University College, twenty-four per cent were killed, and at Corpus Christi, twenty-five per cent. These men suffered disproportionately because they were generally quick to enlist, were fit enough to be placed in the front line, and in many cases, served as junior officers leading their men in offensive operations. By contrast, the casualty rate among working men from Oxford University

Serving members of the Oxford City Police, November 1915. These men were, from left to right: standing, PCs Fowler, Gardner, Grimsley, Atkins; seated, PCs Dunkley, Viner, Bliss. Of the forty-one police officers who enlisted during the war, four were killed and four returned 'much broken in health'.

Press, 45 (12.6 per cent) out of 356 who served in the war, was close to the national average. The City Police lost four (9.8 per cent) out of forty-one serving officers, a lower proportion perhaps because some of them became military police behind the lines.

The scale of the conflict led to acts of remembrance from the early days of the war. New College held a memorial service at the end of Michaelmas Term 1914, when the Warden, the Rev W.A. Spooner, read out the names of fallen members of the college, including the German Prince Wohsch of Welbeck who had been shot while trying to bring in wounded men. This aroused some discord within the college and there was public controversy in 1915 when a Roll of Honour was placed in the College Chapel, including the names of Germans who had died for their country. An American wrote to the *Morning Post* criticising the college, and H.W.B. Joseph tried to persuade a *Daily Mail* journalist to drop the subject. The Warden robustly defended the position of the college, arguing that 'to attempt to carry an aspect of hate against those who have passed into another world can make us neither better patriots nor better men'.

A choral concert to remember the fallen was held at the Sheldonian Theatre in February 1915, including Verdi's *Requiem* and Sir Hubert Parry's *The Glories of Our Blood and State*. In November 1915 a memorial service for Oxford citizens killed in the war was held at All Saints, the city church, and eighteen men from St Clement's were remembered at a service in the parish church in January 1916. New College commemorated Arthur Heath and George Cheesman, 'as good a pair of tutors as any college could hope to have', at a service in October 1915, and Brasenose College held a memorial service for the fifty-eight members who had already died in November 1916. Magdalen College kept a roll of honour in the Chapel, a tablet on which the names inscribed were surrounded by bay leaves; another lily, the college emblem, was entwined in these leaves as each name was added.

Rev A.C. Scott, Vicar of St Mary and St John parish, unveils a war shrine at 34 Essex Street, March 1917. The oak-framed roll of honour listed forty-seven men who were serving in the forces, five of whom had already been killed.

The anniversary of the outbreak of the war became a focus for remembrance, and in August 1918, for example, discharged soldiers and sailors from Holy Trinity parish in Oxford, paraded in Albion Place, and marched through the streets to a special service in the parish church.

Although the British war dead could not be repatriated, local cemeteries soon held the graves of servicemen and women who died of their injuries in hospital or fell victim to illness or accidents. Military funeral processions from the Third Southern General Hospital to Botley

Discharged soldiers march through the streets of St Ebbe's, August 1918. They were on their way to a special remembrance service in Holy Trinity Church where a memorial to the ninety parishioners killed in the war was unveiled in 1920.

Cemetery became a regular sight; the cemetery contains 156 Great War burials, including Australians, Belgians, Canadians, New Zealanders and a South African. Four Germans are also buried there and one staff nurse, Mabel Murray, from the Third Southern General Hospital who died of pneumonia following influenza. Many British casualties who died in the Oxford war hospitals were taken back to their home parishes for burial, and some of Oxford's war dead were buried in local cemeteries and churchyards. Osney Cemetery, for example, contains the grave of Lance Corporal Henry Randall of the Royal Berkshire Regiment, who died on 3 January 1916, one of the three sons Mrs Randall lost in the war. Some of the victims of flying accidents from Port Meadow aerodrome were buried at Wolvercote Cemetery and plots were reserved at Rose Hill Cemetery for deaths from the Ashhurst War Hospital.

Relatives, friends, neighbours and colleagues of the dead increasingly felt the need to record their sacrifice in some physical way. Few permanent memorials were erected during the war, and Oriel College decided as early as November 1914 not to permit individual memorials to its members in the college chapel. The Bishop of Oxford tried to discourage them across the Diocese, preferring post-war corporate memorials of appropriate design. A tablet to Private Lawrence Edwards, of the Royal Army Medical Corps, killed when the hospital ship, *Lanfranc*, was torpedoed on 17 April 1917, is a rare wartime example in St Frideswide's Church.

Early in 1916 two large boards were erected outside the Oxford University Press bearing the names of employees who were serving, and picking out with bands of crepe those who had been killed. Across Oxford, local communities and parishes, backed by Anglican clergymen, set up war shrines and created rolls of honour as permanent memorials. The first war shrines were glazed oak frames containing a list of the serving men and the fallen from the immediate neighbourhood. Later ones were sometimes more elaborately crafted and might feature hinged panels, a shelf for flowers, and even, at St Barnabas' Church in 1919, praying stools beneath an altar displaying framed photographs. The first local war shrine was unveiled at Banbury in October 1916, and the town had several more before the first Oxford one was consecrated by the Archdeacon of Oxford in Randolph Street in January 1917. Listing the names of thirty-nine serving men, it demonstrated the extent of the war's reach into this little street off Cowley Road.

A second shrine, funded by a public subscription, was unveiled on the wall of 118 Howard Street, a serving soldier's home, in March. This recorded the names of 100 men from the area, seven of whom had been killed. Further shrines were placed in Divinity Road, Essex Street, Hertford Street, Leopold Street, Magdalen Road, Percy Street and Southfield Road. Given the Catholic character of these shrines, it is perhaps no coincidence that all were located in the High Church parish of SS Mary and John. Another war shrine was erected on the south wall of the High Anglican church, St Barnabas', in January 1919, but a shrine at St Ebbe's Church and a simple framed list in Caroline Street, St Clement's showed that Evangelical parishes shared the desire to commemorate the fallen publicly. At Holy Trinity in St Ebbe's, a metal plaque bearing the names of the ninety parishioners who had been killed in the war was dedicated in the church in May 1920.

Memorial halls were described by the *Oxford Journal Illustrated* as being a much more useful form of war memorial than war shrines. The Iffley Institute and Reading Room, opened in June 1917, was founded by Sir George Forrest, a retired Indian Civil Servant, and supported by the local businessman, John Allen. It provided a library and writing-room in one building, and a separate reading room containing framed lists of serving and killed parishioners. *The Times* reported in July 1917 that its purpose was…

> 'to commemorate alike the brave sons of the village who died fighting for England, and the gallant survivors who shared their dangers, toils and sufferings. To show honour to the dead and gratitude to the living by a Memorial whose object is to imbue successive generations with the same love of country and sense of duty, and to forge, by the memory of valour and self-donation, a fresh bond of union and friendship among all who dwell in this ancient village.'

In December 1917, the first of a series of musical evenings was held at the Institute, and Sir George emphasised the following October that it was open to all wounded soldiers. By the time the Institute celebrated its fourth anniversary in July 1921 with a concert and 'moonlight dancing', the young men and women of the village were said to regard it as 'their club'. After the war in April 1920 the people of Summertown followed Iffley's example and decided to build a hall in Banbury Road as the best possible memorial to dead parishioners.

Each Oxford college had to decide how best to commemorate its lost undergraduates and other members. As early as November 1914, Oriel College decided that no memorials to individuals killed in the war would be erected in the Chapel. Trinity College was considering a memorial brass or tablet in October 1915, and a volume of photographs and tributes by summer 1917. Mr Justice Higgins gave Balliol £500 towards the war memorial fund in memory of his son in March 1918, and in October,the college was still asking old members what form the memorial should take. Their suggestions included improvements to the Chapel interior, the endowment of a Poor Students' Fund and scholarships in modern subjects. Most colleges eventually opted for a Roll of Honour, listing the names of all the fallen.

In 1921 the Christ Church memorial tablets, recording just names and honours, were placed in the cathedral passage and the New College memorial to its Allied war dead was unveiled in the Ante-Chapel. Nine years later, and following Warden Spooner's lead in 1915, a small plaque was added nearby, recording the three German members of the college who died in the war. At Magdalen, the memorial plaques are in the Chapel porch, and, reflecting President Warren's view of the College as a community, the list is purely alphabetical, omitting military ranks and civilian status, and including the jobbing bricklayer among the college servants.

Magdalen College also erected a memorial cross in St John's Quadrangle in 1921, ignoring the objections of one college fellow, Robert Gunther, who condemned it as 'a phallus with a silly little cross at the top'. Other forms of commemoration included a fellowship and memorial volumes at Balliol, college libraries at Trinity and New College and the Memorial Garden at Christ Church laid out in 1927.

The University, the University Press and some colleges and private schools published war records as another way of commemorating service and sacrifice. *The Oxford University Roll of Service* published in 1920 contained the names of all 14,561 members of the University who served in the armed forces, highlighting those who had been

Remembrance Day at Carfax, 11 November 1920. The crowd brought traffic to a halt during the two minutes' silence on the second anniversary of the Armistice. A laurel wreath bearing the inscription 'In honoured memory of our fallen Comrades of the Great War' was attached to the central lamp standard.

killed, and including the citation for winners of the Victoria Cross. Sixteen University men had been awarded the highest gallantry award during the War, and VCs had also been awarded to two Oxford men, Dudley Johnson and John Smyth, as well as to Company Sergeant Major Edward Brooks and Lance Corporal Alfred Wilcox of the 2/4th Battalion Oxfordshire and Buckinghamshire Light Infantry. (Appendix Table 3)

Alderman Sir Robert Buckell, Mayor of Oxford, proposed setting up a committee to start fund-raising for a war memorial in October

1916. He went on to chair the War Museum Committee which was formed in June 1917, and set out to create what would have been a local version of the Imperial War Museum. In January 1919 the City Council referred the now pressing issue of a war memorial to the committee, and Henry Hare, the architect of Oxford Town Hall, proposed a Memorial Hall on a site in St Giles' owned by St John's College. The public were asked for ideas and came up with many suggestions – removing the cattle market from Gloucester Green, providing cottages for disabled servicemen, erecting a central hall and pleasure grounds, even placing a Time Ball on the Radcliffe Observatory tower. St John's College vetoed Hare's Memorial Hall in

Unveiling the Oxford War Memorial in St Giles' on 9 July 1921. After much debate about the form the memorial should take, and where it should be, this large granite cross was erected south of St Giles's Church. It commemorates the sacrifice of both the City and the University.

April 1919 because it would block views of St Giles's Church, but welcomed the alternative proposal for a tall granite cross, and offered the site as a free gift. J.E. Thorpe won the competition to design the cross and the committee asked two other local architects, G.T. Gardner and Thomas Rayson, to help work up the final designs. Some people wanted the memorial placed in the centre of St Giles', but a local referendum produced a majority in favour of the site south of St Giles's Church.

Between seven and eight thousand people were present when the Oxford War Memorial, consciously designed as a Town and Gown tribute, was unveiled on 9 July 1921. The *Oxford Chronicle* felt that the huge interest…

> 'spoke eloquently of the sad memories that haunt hundreds of homes, and the gratitude that is kept burning in the hearts of all for the men who made the supreme sacrifice.'

Approximately one in five British families lost a close relative, and some of course experienced multiple tragedies. Mrs Randall in Abbey Place lost three sons, and the Jamiesons in Charles Street lost two. Vera Brittain lost both her fiancé, Roland Leighton and her brother, Edward. Reginald Macan, Master of University College, recorded his thoughts about his son on what would have been his thirty-third birthday:

> 'Basil must ever be the gallant man, in the prime of life, picture of health, strength, courage, calm, and manliness, who was killed by that shell, on Sunday morning, 9.30 in the salient at Ypres, 1915, June 13… Alas what hopes, and possibilities lie buried in that grave! How do we survive these unspeakable disasters?'

Relatives' replies to letters of consolation from Sir Herbert Warren, President of Magdalen College, expose their grief and show how they were trying to cope. Cecil Fleet, widowed when her husband, William, was killed in May 1918, comforted herself with precious memories of their few happy months together. In April 1916, Reginald Farrar and his wife commented on the death of their son, Valentine, in the trenches: 'Our loss is indeed grievous, but there is some pride in having given so fine so gifted so gallant a son in our dear country's cause.'

Patriotism also provided solace for C.R.L. Fletcher when his son, Reginald, was killed in 1915:

'In honest truth, I have no doubt, nor has his mother any doubt, that he particularly <u>enjoyed</u> the war and that the last six weeks of his life were the happiest of a very happy life.'

Three days before he died, Reginald had written:

'Thank God we have a <u>Cause</u> to fight for – not like those poor lambs of Germans driven to the slaughter to satisfy the ambitions of a few swollen-headed vampires.'

Brigadier General Robert White, introducing Major Rose's *Story of the 2/4th Oxfordshire and Buckinghamshire Light Infantry* in 1920, echoed the Fletchers' positive view of the war. He described 'the wonderful years during which we ceased to be individuals, pursuing the ordinary avocations of life and became indeed a band of brothers, linked together in a common cause...' He recalled 'the hopes and fears, the pathos and fun, the excitements and the weariness, and the hundred other emotions which gave to life in the Great War a sense of adventure which we can hardly hope to savour again.'

Such sentiments were not widely shared in the post-war years. Replying to a request for stories about the war, a University Press man remarked that they would prefer to say little or nothing:

'Indeed, some things are better forgotten. I wish I could forget some, but it seems that the more gruesome and horrible things cling to you, and take some shaking off.'

War trophies became an unappreciated part of remembrance as the government rewarded institutions that had assisted the war effort with captured ordnance. Five German guns, a 16-pounder and four 12-pounders, were brought to Oxford on 1 December 1918 and exhibited in St Giles' after a civic procession from the GWR goods station. One of these guns was later placed in the Botanic Garden and became a focus for undergraduate mischief. On Remembrance Day in 1919, it was dragged down to Folly Bridge and run into the river. Undergraduates hauled the gun away again on 5 November 1920 but police intercepted them in High Street and reclaimed it. The War Office offered the University a German field gun in January 1919 in appreciation of the work of the Officer Training Corps, and Balliol, Lincoln and University were among the colleges which received captured guns. Balliol College placed their trophy in the Fellows'

Garden, but undergraduates soon heaved it over the wall into the cucumber frame in the President of Trinity's garden. Lincoln's gun was soon exiled to the college cricket field and was offered for scrap in 1940 when a new conflict probably claimed any surviving trophies.

In November 1914, the Right Rev Charles Gore, Bishop of Oxford, expressed the view that 'we've done magnificently the right thing in going to war with Germany and Austria,' but he warned that the success of post-war reconstruction would depend very much on how it was motivated:

> 'If it is allowed to take place under the motives of revenge, jealousy, and the balance of power, it will be reconstruction only leading up to a new collapse.'

A war which took out a whole generation of jurists, scholars, administrators and political leaders resulted in just such a peace

Patients celebrate peace at the Wingfield Hospital in Headington, July 1919. They had paraded the streets in fancy dress, not their usual blue hospital uniforms, with the message, 'Wake Up Oxford, Peace Is Signed'.

settlement, and sowed the seeds for an even worse conflagration. None of this seemed to worry the crowds who poured into the streets of Oxford again to celebrate the signing of the Treaty of Versailles on 28 June 1919. Some people wore huge Union Jacks, men wore women's hats decorated with patriotic colours, and wounded soldiers marched through the crowd singing popular songs: 'Jollifications increased as the evening wore on, and everyone enjoyed the fun, especially the "flappers", who were out in force.' The Great War was truly at an end, and Oxford stood, quite unwittingly, on the brink of becoming an industrial city.

Appendix 1: Tables

TABLE 1   CITY OF OXFORD: AGE STRUCTURE, 1901

Ages	Males	Females	Persons
0-4	2390	2352	4742
5-9	2357	2358	4715
10-14	2601	2589	5190
15-19	2245	3002	5247
20-29	3512	5378	8890
30-39	2903	3977	6880
40-49	2369	3013	5382
50-59	1732	2309	4041
60-69	1092	1550	2642
70-79	505	750	1255
80-89	115	220	335
90-99	6	11	17
	21827	27509	49336

TABLE 2   CITY OF OXFORD: OCCUPATION STRUCTURE, 1901

Males	Occupations	Females
317	National and Local Government	29
129	Defence	0
1062	Professions	818
1303	Domestic Service	4982
694	Commercial	76
1863	Transport	28
376	Agriculture	8
1	Fishing	0
64	Mines and Quarries	5
605	Metals and Machines	5
210	Jewels and Instruments	7
1850	Building and Construction	2
402	Wood and Furniture	36
51	Brick Cement and Glass	4
76	Chemicals	7
58	Skins and Leather	10
880	Paper and Printing	155
170	Textiles	253
921	Tailoring and Dress	1629
1527	Food Drink and Inns	698
118	Gas Water and Electricity	
921	Other Workers and Dealers	131
13598	Total	8883
449	Retired	153
170	Living on own means	1040

TABLE 3: OXFORD MEN AWARDED THE VICTORIA CROSS
DURING THE GREAT WAR

Name	Rank	College	Regiment	Date
Edward Brooks	C S M		Oxfordshire & Buckinghamshire L I	28.4.17
Angus Buchanan	Temp/Captain	Jesus	South Wales Borderers	5.4.16
Christopher Bushnell	Lt Colonel	Corpus Christi	Queen's (Royal West Surrey)	23.3.18
Adrian Carton de Wiart	Lt Colonel	Balliol	4th Royal Irish Dragoon Guards	2-3.7.16
Noel Chavasse	Captain	Trinity	Royal Army Medical Corps	9.8.16; 31.7.17- 2.8.17
John Collings-Wells	Act/Lt Colonel	Christ Church	Bedfordshire	22-27.3.18
Geoffrey Drummond	Lieutenant	Christ Church	Royal Naval Volunteer Reserve	9-10.5.18
Thomas Colyer Ferguson	Act/Captain	Oriel	Northamptonshire	31.7.17
Benjamin Geary	2nd Lieutenant	Keble	1st East Surrey	20-21.4.15
David Hirsch	Act/Captain	Worcester	Green Howards	23.4.17
Dudley Johnson	Captain		Royal Sussex	4.11.18
John Aidan Liddell	Captain	Balliol	Argyll & Sutherland Highlanders, attached to Royal Flying Corps	31.7.15
Eric McNair	Temp/Lieutenant	Magdalen	Royal Sussex	14.2.16
George Maling	Lieutenant	Exeter	Royal Army Medical Corps	25.9. 15
John Smyth	Lieutenant		15th Ludhiana Sikhs, Indian Army	18.5.15
Charles Vickers	Temp/Captain	Merton	Sherwood Foresters	14.10.15
Garth Walford	Captain	Balliol	Royal Artillery	26.4.15
Frank Wearne	2nd Lieutenant	Corpus Christi	Essex	28.6.17
Alfred Wilcox	L/Corporal		Oxfordshire & Buckinghamshire L I	12.9.18
Geoffrey Woolley	2nd Lieutenant	Queen's	Queen Victoria's Rifles	20-21.4.15

Appendix 2:

Oxford in the Great War timeline

August 1914 – War Declared
13 August 1914 – Oxford Volunteer Corps, a Dad's Army, holds its first drill in the University Parks
23 August 1914 – British Army in action at Battle of Mons
13 September 1914 – First batch of wounded soldiers arrives at Third Southern General Hospital
7 November 1914 – Belgian Day, Oxford's first large-scale Flag Day
11 November 1914 – Oxfordshire & Buckinghamshire Light Infantry action in Nonne Bosschen Wood, Ypres
19 January 1915 – First Zeppelin raid on Great Britain
10-13 March 1915 – Battle of Neuve Chapelle
April 1915 – January 1916 – Gallipoli campaign
20-21 April 1915 – Benjamin Geary and Geoffrey Woolley, the first University men awarded Victoria Cross during the war
April – 25 May – Second Battle of Ypres and first use of poison gas by German Army
7 May 1915 – *Lusitania* sunk by German U-boat
25-28 September – Battle of Loos
2 October 1915 – Great Military rally to boost recruiting in Oxford
7 March 1916 – First air raid warning in Oxford, a false alarm
29 April 1916 – Serbian refugees arrive in Oxford
31 May - June 1, 1916 – Battle of Jutland
1 July 1916 – First Day of the Battle of the Somme
21 November 1916 – Battle of the Somme ends
28 January 1917 – First Oxford war shrine unveiled, in Randolph Street
29 March 1917 – Policewoman, Grace Costin, appointed to curb indecent behaviour in the streets
6 April 1917 – USA declares war on Germany
28 April 1917 – Company Sergeant Major Edward Brooks, Oxfordshire & Buckinghamshire Light Infantry, awarded Victoria Cross

17 May 1917 – First War Kitchen opens in Cambridge Terrace

6 July 1917 – Arab rebels led by Lawrence of Arabia capture Aqaba

31 July – 10 November 1917 – Third Battle of Ypres (Passchendaele)

31 July – 2 August 1917 – Captain Noel Chavasse, Royal Army Medical Corps, awarded second, posthumous Victoria Cross

11 March 1918 – Compulsory food rationing introduced in Oxford

21 March 1918 – Germany launches the Spring Offensive

1 April 1918 – The Royal Air Force founded

8 August 1918 – The Hundred Days offensive begins on The Western Front

11 November 1918 – Germany signs the Armistice ending the fighting at 11am

11 November 1918 – Emperors' heads on Sheldonian Theatre painted red on Armistice Day

19 June 1919 – 'Oriel raid' on Somerville undergraduates in St Mary Hall Quad

28 June 1919 – Peace celebrations to mark signing of Treaty of Versailles

9 July 1921 – Unveiling of Oxford War Memorial

Bibliography

Printed sources

Pauline Adams, *Somerville for Women: an Oxford College, 1879-1993* (1996)

Mark Adkin, *The Western Front Companion* (2013)

P.W.S. Andrews & Elizabeth Brunner, *The Life of Lord Nuffield* (1959)

Max Arthur, *Forgotten Voices of the Great War* (2003)

Michael Asher, *Lawrence: the Uncrowned King of Arabia* (1998)

David Bilton, *The Home Front in the Great War: Aspects of the Conflict, 1914-1918* (2003)

Geoffrey Bolton, *History of the OUCC* (1962)

Vera Brittain, Testament of Youth: an Autobiographical Study of the Years 1900-1925 (1979)

Ibid., War Diary 1913-1917: Chronicles of Youth (1981)

Ibid., The Women at Oxford (1960)

L.W.B. Brockliss, *Magdalen College, Oxford: a History* (2008)

Barry Burnham, *The Forgotten Dead: the Men of Holy Trinity Parish, Oxford, Who Died in the Great War* (2010)

C.V. Butler, *Social Conditions in Oxford* (1912)

Joanna Cannan, *High Table* (1987)

M.V. Cannan, *Grey Ghosts and Voices* (1976)

Jeremy Catto, *ed., Oriel College: A History* (2013)

Ann Clayton, *Chavasse – Double VC* (1992)

E.S. Craig, *ed., Oxford University Roll of Service* (1920)

J.M. Crook, *Brasenose: the Biography of an Oxford College* (2008)

R.B. Crosse, *A Short History of the Oxfordshire and Buckinghamshire Light Infantry, 1741-1922* (1944)

Alan Crossley, *ed., Victoria History of the County of Oxford, vol. 4: the City of Oxford* (1979)

Judith Curthoys, *The Cardinal's College: Christ Church, Chapter and Verse* (2012)

Robin Darwall-Smith, *A History of University College* (2008)

H.R. Davies, Cowley Barracks during the Great War, 1914-1919, in, *Bugle and Sabre*, vol. 1 (2007)

Ken Delve, *The Military Airfields of Britain: Northern Home Counties* (2007)

J.N. Dykes, *Reminiscences of a Soldier Training in Oxford 1915* (1976)

David Eddershaw, *The Story of the Oxfordshire Yeomanry: Queen's Own Oxfordshire Hussars 1798-1998* (1998)

J.M. Falkner, *A History of Oxfordshire* (1899)

C.R.L. Fletcher, *A Handy Guide to Oxford, Specially Written for the Wounded* (1915)

Colin Fox, *Responding to the Call: the Kitchener Battalions of the Royal Berkshire Regiment 1915* (1995)

Robert Fox & Graeme Gooday, *Physics at Oxford 1839-1939* (2005)

Paul Fussell, *The Great War and Modern Memory* (1975)

Martin Gilbert, *The First World War: A Complete History* (1994)

Jocelyn Goddard, *Mixed Feelings: Littlemore Hospital – an Oral History Project* (1996)

Malcolm Graham, *Diverse Oxfordshire* (2010)

Ibid., Images of Victorian Oxford (1992)

Ibid., Oxford Heritage Walk 2 (2014)

Ibid., Oxford Yesterday and Today (1997)

Ibid., The Suburbs of Victorian Oxford (1985)

Frank Gray, *The Confessions of a Private* (1920)

V.H.H Green, *The Commonwealth of Lincoln College, 1427-1977* (1979)

G.B. Grundy, *Fifty-five Years at Oxford* (1945)

Martin Harris, *Nuffield Orthopaedic Centre: a Pictorial History* (2011)

Simon Harris, *History of the 43rd and 52nd (Oxfordshire and Buckinghamshire) Light Infantry in the Great War, vol. 2: The 52nd Light Infantry in France and Flanders* (2012)

Brian Harrison, *ed., History of the University of Oxford, vol. 8: the Twentieth Century* (1994)

Christopher Hibbert , *ed., The Encyclopaedia of Oxford* (1988)

Tanis Hinchcliffe, *North Oxford* (1992)

Richard Holmes, *Tommy: the British Soldier on the Western Front, 1914-1918* (2005)

Clare Hopkins, *Trinity: 450 Years of an Oxford College Community* (2005)

John Horne, *ed., A Companion to World War 1* (2012)

D.R. Johnstone-Jones, Some Other Yanks at Oxford, in, *Oxford* 33/1 (May 1981)

John Jones, *Balliol College: a History*, 2nd ed (2005)

H.W.B. Joseph, Memorials of Oxford Men: John Scott Haldane, in, *Oxford* 3/1 (1936)

Elaine Kaye, *Mansfield College: its Origin, History and Significance* (1996)

Adrian Keith-Falconer, *The Oxfordshire Hussars in the Great War, 1914-1918* (1927)

Anthony Kenny, ed., *The History of the Rhodes Trust, 1902-1999* (2001)

J.B. Langstaff, *Oxford – 1914* (1965)

G.T. Launchbury, John Allen & Sons (Oxford) Ltd., 1868-1952, in, *Allen's Activities* 14 (Spring 1953)

Dino Lemonofides, The formation of the OTC, in, *Bugle and Sabre*, vol. 2 (2008)

M.D. Lobel, ed., *Victoria History of the County of Oxford, vol. 5: Bullingdon Hundred* (1957)

E.C. Lodge, *Terms and Vacations* (1938)

W.R. Lovis, ed., *The History of Oxford University Press, vol. 3, 1896-1970* (2013)

Peter Maasz, The Oxfordshire Hussars at Rifle Wood, in, *Bugle and Sabre*, vol. 2 (2008)

Martin McIntyre, *The Royal Berkshire Regiment, 1914-1959* (2005)

J.R. Maddicott, An Infinitesimal Part in Armageddon: Exeter College and the First World War, in, *Exeter College Association Register* (1998)

Frederic Manning, *Her Privates We* (1986)

G.H. Martin & J.R.L. Highfield, *A History of Merton College* (1997)

James Munson, ed., *Echoes of the Great War: the Diary of the Rev Andrew Clark, 1914-1919* (1988)

J.E.H. Neville, *History of the 43rd and 52nd (Oxfordshire and Buckinghamshire) Light Infantry in the Great War, vol. 1: the 43rd Light Infantry in Mesopotamia and North Russia* (1938)

Sir Rex Niven, Balliol in 1916-17, in *Balliol College Record* (1984)

Kevin Northover, *Banbury in the Great War* (2003)

R.J. Overy, *William Morris, Lord Nuffield* (1976)

Oxford & Swindon Co-operative Society, *A History of a Hundred Years Co-operation in Oxford* (1972)

Oxford City Council, *Housing Scheme: the Present Financial Position* (1928)

Ibid., Report of Oxford War Memorial Committee (1921)

Oxford Preservation Trust, *Shopping in Oxford: a Brief History* (1983)

Oxfordshire & Buckinghamshire Light Infantry, Roll of Honour 1914-1919 (1931?)

William Page, ed., *Victoria History of the County of Oxford*, vol. 2 (1907)

P. Pickford, *War Record of the 1/4th Battalion Oxfordshire and Buckinghamshire Light Infantry* (1919)

Leonard Rice-Oxley, *Oxford in Arms, with an Account of Keble College* (1917)

Ibid., Oxford in Arms, with an Account of New College (1918)

A.H.T. Robb-Smith, *A Short History of the Radcliffe Infirmary* (1970)

G K Rose, The Story of the 2/4th Oxfordshire and Buckinghamshire Light Infantry (1920)

Raphael Samuel, ed., *Village Life and Labour* (1975)

Laura Schwartz, *A Serious Endeavour: Gender, Education and Community at St Hugh's, 1886-2011* (2011)

Ben Shephard, The Nerve Doctors, in *Oxford Today* 12/3 (Trinity 2000),

W.T.S Stallybrass, Oxford 1914-1918, in *Oxford* 16 /2 (Winter 1939)

John Stevenson, Government, Oxford and Oriel, 1914-1990, in Jeremy Catto, *ed., Oriel College: a History* (2013)

Lawrence Stone, ed., *The University in Society, vol.1* (1974)

Norman Stone, *World War One: a Short History* (2007)

Victor Sugden, *An Oxford Diary* (1992)

Anne Summers, *Oxfordshire in the First World War* (1978)

P.H. Sutcliffe, *The Oxford University Press: an Informal History* (1978)

Henry Taunt, *Oxford Illustrated by Camera and Pen* (1911?)

Reginald Thomas, *The Bells of Heaven Go Ting-a-Ling-a-Ling* (1976)

William Tuckwell, *Reminiscences of Oxford* (1900)

Christopher Tyerman, *New College* (2010)

Univ in the First World War, in *University College Record* (1984)

Stuart Wallace, *War and the Image of Germany: British Academics 1914-1918* (1988)

War Record of the University Press, Oxford (1923)

Laurence Waters, *Oxfordshire Railways in Old Photographs* (1989)

C. Wheeler, *Memorial Record of the 7th (Service) Battalion The*

Oxfordshire and Buckinghamshire Light Infantry (1921)
Michael White, *Tolkien: a Biography* (2001)
J.M. Winter, Oxford and the First World War, in Brian Harrison, ed., *History of the University of Oxford, vol. 8: the Twentieth Century* (1994)

Online resources

Commonwealth War Graves Commission – http://www.cwgc.org/
First World War Poetry Digital Archive – http:/www.oucs.ox.ac.uk/ww1lit/
Oxford Dictionary of National Biography – http://www.oxforddnb/com/

Serials

(see also Manuscript sources)
Annual Reports of the Chief Constable of the City of Oxford
Annual Reports of the Medical Officer of Health for the City of Oxford
Balliol College Record
Bugle and Sabre
Clarendonian
The Club at War: War Edition of the Balliol Boys' Club Magazine
Exeter College Association Register
The Listener
Oliver's Oxford Almanack
Orthopaedic Life
Oxford
Oxford Chronicle
Oxford Diocesan Magazine
Oxford Journal Illustrated
Oxford Magazine
Oxford Mail
The Oxford Times
Oxford Today
Oxfordshire and Buckinghamshire Light Infantry Chronicle
Pelican Record
Stapeldon Magazine
The Times
The Varsity
University College Record

Manuscript sources

Balliol College

05-187-003a J.H. Brian Armstrong, Album re no. 6 Officer Cadet Battalion, 1917

English Register, Minute Book of Masters and Fellows, 1908-24

Bodleian Libraries

(a) Special Collections

MS Eng hist e.93, Andrew Clark, War Diary: Oxford visits, 1914

MS Eng Hist e.100, Andrew Clark, War Diary: Oxford visits, 1915

MS Eng Misc d.790, Hilda Pickard-Cambridge, August MCMXIV

MSS Eng Misc e.826-7, Isabel Dixey, Diary, 1915-6

MS Top Oxon c.247-8, Belgian Refugee Committee Registers

MS Top Oxon c.326, A.B. Poynton, The Effects of the War on Oxford

MS Top Oxon d.239, Anglo-German Society Minutes, 1912-14

MS Top Oxon d.563, Rachael Poole, Oxford in War Time, 1918

MS Top Oxon d.664, Hilda Pickard-Cambridge, Oxford During the War, vol. 4, 1917-18

MS Top Oxon d. 665, Hilda Pickard-Cambridge, Balliol War memorial, vol. 2

MS Top Oxon d.903, University Museum Social Evening Committee Minutes, 1919

MS Top Oxon e.193, Belgian Refugees Committee Minute Book, 1914-15

MS Top Oxon e.288, H.W.B. Joseph, Diary, 1914-18

MS Top Oxon e. 529, Corporal A.R. Wilkins, Diary of the late 128th (Oxon) Heavy Battery, 1916-18

(b) John Johnson Collection

Great War Boxes 3, 17, 20

(c) Oxford University Archives

LHD/L/5/3, Termly statistics of lodging-houses, 1911-20

LHD/SF/8/1, Papers concerning World War One

LHD/SF/8/2, Compensation correspondence, 1914-15

PR1/23/4/1, Proctors' Book Names, 1910-20

VC1/43, Vice-Chancellor's correspondence, 1918-19

Corpus Christi College

B/4/1/11-12, Governing Body Minutes, 1907-16, 1916-22

B/14/1/1/36, Thomas Case, Report of the President..., 1914

B/17/4/2, Letters to Thomas Case

Magdalen College

PR/2/18-19, President's Note book, 1913-17, 1917-21

PR32/C3, Incoming Letters from Members on Active Service

Oriel College

Gov 4.A7-8, Governing Body Minutes, 1913-18, 1918-26

TF2 B8/1 Treasurer's records, 1914-18

Oriel Record

Oxford University Press

PR/22/2/1, University Press Scrapbook

Clarendonian

Oxfordshire History Centre

CC 2.29, Oxford City Cemeteries Committee Minutes, 1880-1915

GG.1.1, Oxford City Playgrounds and Bathing Places Committee Minutes, 1914-19

GG.4.3, Oxford City Special Committees Minutes, 1914-23

H1/CV1/A1/6 Littlemore Asylum Committee of Visitors Minute Book, 1913-31

HH.4.3, Oxford Citizens' Emergency Committee Minutes, 1915-23

HH.4.16, Oxford Pig-Rearing and Public Health Sub-Committees, 1917-18

HH.4.21, Oxford City War Executive Committee Minutes, 1914-15

HH.4.30, Oxford Relief Committee Minutes, 1914-23

O11/1/N1/1, County of Oxford Territorial Force Association, Report of Administration, 1908-13

POL 1/1/N1/5, Oxford City Police Newscuttings, 1916-19

S76/5/A1/2, Cowley St John Boys' School log book 1902-44

S76/6/A1/2, Cowley St John Girls' School log book, 1908-59

S127/1/A2/3 Headington Quarry School log book 1914-19

S165/1/A1/2, Marston Church of England School log book, 1890-1922

S198/3/A1/2, St Clement's Girls' School log book, 1907-29

S202/1/A1/3, St Frideswide's Boys' School log book, 1914-30

S261/1/A1/3, Summertown Mixed School log book, 1904-25

Robert Buckell, Mayor of Oxford's correspondence, 1916/7

Henry Taunt, Jingles, c. 1915

St Hilda's College

2007.0012 Margot Collinson letters, 1917-20

BURR029/17, Oxford Women's War Service Committee, 1915-16

BURR029/18, City of Oxford Emergency Committee: Report of Sub-Committees, 1914-16

BURR029/38, M.G. Carden, Women Patrols

BURR031/68-9, Lady Margaret Hall Report, 1916/17-1917/18

BURR 031/72, St Hugh's College, 1916/17- 1917/18

BURR 031/74, Society of Home Students, 1917-18

BURR 031/84, Somerville College Report and Calendar, 1916/17-1917/18

CH/MF02-05a, Cherwell Hall Magazine, 1914-18

MIN 013/1, General Meeting Minutes, 1910-18

PUB 001/17-21, St Hilda's Hall Report, 1914/15-1918/19

PUB002/9-13, Chronicle of Old Students' Association, 1914-18

REF 010/48-61, The Fritillary, 1914-18

SA1/A1-2, 9, Oral History interviews

St John's College

Admin I. A.10, Register, 1861-1930

Admin II.A.2, Estates Committee Minutes, 1869-1932

Photographs 211, Alexander Kleinwort Album, 1912-13

Somerville College

SC/L7/AR/WW1/6, Move to Oriel and back, 1915-19

SC/L7/AR/WW1/7, Reminiscences of Oriel Raid, 1919

1914-1918 Box

Penrose 2 Box

Somerville Students' Association, Annual Report & Oxford Letter, 1914-20

University College

MA43/J1/5, Reginald Macan, Diary, 1915

MA43/J1/6, Mildred Macan, Diary, 1918-22

S20/MS1/1-2, F.C. Conybeare letter and report

Oxford in the Great War: Key to Map Numbers

1. Somerville Section, 3rd Southern General Hospital

2. Voluntary Aid Detachment Hospital, 23 Banbury Road

3. School of Aeronautics, Royal Flying Corps, University Museum

4. Red Cross Working Party, School of Forestry, Parks Road

5. Mansfield College Garden Club

6. Headquarters, 4th Battalion Oxfordshire & Buckinghamshire Light Infantry

7. New College Garden, 3rd Southern General Hospital

8. Masonic Buildings, 3rd Southern General Hospital

9. Examination Schools, 3rd Southern General Hospital

10. University College, 3rd Southern General Hospital

11. Recruiting Office, 90 High Street

12. 3rd Southern General Hospital Nurses' Home, Merton College

13. Somerville College in exile, Oriel College

14. Voluntary Organisations Depot, 22 High Street

15. Catholic Soldiers' Club, 12 Turl Street

16. War Savings Office, 15 Broad Street

17. Young Men's Christian Association Club, 10 George Street

18. Oxfordshire Prisoners of War Fund Office, 4 Magdalen Street

19. Belgian boys' school, St John's College

20. Young Women's Christian Association Club, 62 St Giles'

21. Belgian refugees' hostel, Ruskin College

22. Food Control Office, 24 St Michael's Street

23. Officer Cadet Battalions Club, Oxford Union

24. Young Men's Christian Association temporary Club, 59-61 Cornmarket Street

25. Soldiers' Club, 43A Queen Street

26. Fuel Overseer's Office, 119 St Aldate's Street

27. Town Hall, 3rd Southern General Hospital

28. Wastepaper Depot, 9A St Aldate's Street

29. Three Feathers Temperance pub, 29-30 St Aldate's Street

30. Army Service Corps Supply Depot, Osney Lane

N.B. Most men's colleges took in recruits, billeted soldiers and Army or Royal Flying Corps officer cadets.

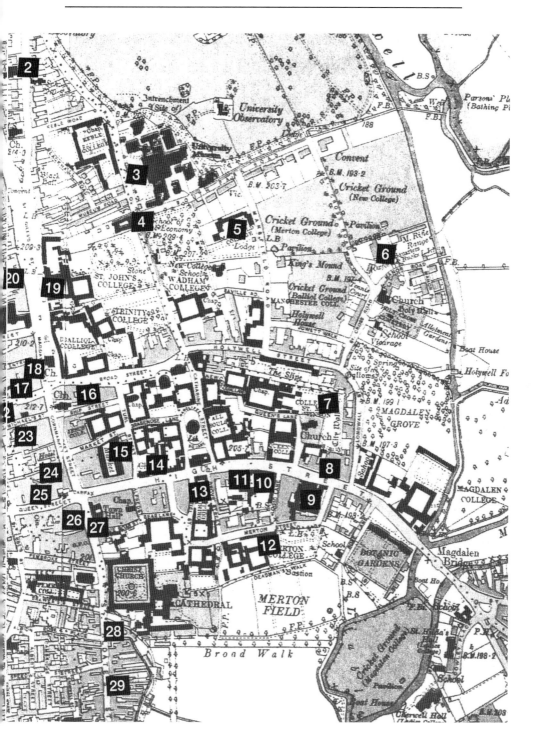

Index